Cybersecurity Fundamentals:

Best Security Practices

By

Bruce Brown, CISSP, ISC2 CGRC

For more details, check out:

http://convocourses.com/courses/bestsecuritypractice

Check us out on:

youtube.com/convocourses

Contact us:

contact@convocourses.com

Contents

INTRODUCTION

My name is Bruce Brown, and I have worked in cybersecurity since 2000. Every week, I meet with the convocourses community, a group interested in sharing information about cybersecurity compliance and IT. Lately, many people have asked me how to get into cybersecurity, possibly due to the growing number of influencers promoting its benefits.

Cybersecurity is an increasingly important field that touches nearly every aspect of our lives. From online banking to social media to government services, we rely on technology to manage and store our most sensitive information. However, this reliance also increases the risk of cyberattacks, data breaches, and threats to national security. Because of this, cybersecurity has exploded in recent years, driven by the growing number of cyberattacks and their consequences.

Companies, governments, and individuals need professionals to protect their networks and systems from cyber threats.

If you're new to the field and want to one day join the ranks of those that protect these systems, this is a good place to start. This book is for people with little or no experience in cybersecurity, but even if you have been an expert for a while, it will provide a refresher on the best security practices.

Security Frameworks Referenced in This Book

Each industry has different mission or business security needs. You're familiar with the financial, healthcare, government (public), and retail sectors, but there are others. This book addresses most of the common best security practices all these sectors need. Each sector has its own set of standards that they need to go by. Here are a few of them:

1. Public Sector (USA): "Public" sector means government. The main security standard the government uses is the National Institute of Standards and Technology (NIST) Risk Management Framework (RMF).

2. Healthcare: The healthcare sector uses the Health Insurance Portability and Accountability Act (HIPAA). Its a U.S. regulation that sets standards for protecting sensitive patient data. The healthcare sector also uses the Health Information Trust Alliance (HITRUST) Common Security Framework (CSF) which is another widely adopted security framework in the healthcare

sector, providing a comprehensive and flexible approach to managing security risks.

3. Financial and Insurance: One of the standards the financial sector uses is the Payment Card Industry Data Security Standard (PCI DSS). It is a set of security standards designed to ensure that companies accepting, processing, storing, or transmitting credit card information maintain a secure environment. Additionally, the Federal Financial Institutions Examination Council (FFIEC) provides guidelines for financial institutions in the United States.

4. Retail: The retail industry commonly uses the PCI DSS to protect credit card information. The National Retail Federation (NRF) also provides cybersecurity resources and best practices for retailers.

5. Hospitality: The hospitality sector often uses the PCI DSS to protect customer credit card information. Some organizations also follow the ISO/IEC 27000 series or the NIST Cybersecurity Framework to secure their information systems.

Another set of controls that are used by these sectors and organizations all over the world is the CIS Critical Security Controls. This book will reference some of these regulations, controls, and standards.

Basic IT Training & Resources

Information technology is foundational to this knowledge. If you know absolutely nothing and you're not familiar with IT or how it works, there will be a lot of concepts you don't understand. Don't worry; you can learn them along the way.

You must work on a common body of knowledge we don't enter in this book. For example, you'll need to know how computers, networks, and cloud technologies work. You will need to know how hardware and software work together and the differences between a client, a server, and a mobile device. At the end of each chapter, we will give resources of places to learn more.

Here is a list of resources you can check out if you are an absolute beginner with computers:

- Khan Academy (https://www.khanacademy.org): Offers free online courses and resources on various IT subjects, including computer programming, algorithms, and computer science principles.

- Coursera (https://www.coursera.org): Provides a wide range of IT courses covering computer basics, programming, web development, and more topics.

- Codecademy (https://www.codecademy.com): Offers interactive online courses on coding, web development, and other IT-related topics.

- edX (https://www.edx.org): Offers IT courses from universities and institutions worldwide, covering subjects like computer science, data analysis, and cybersecurity.

- W3Schools (https://www.w3schools.com): A web development tutorial website that covers HTML, CSS, JavaScript, and other web technologies.

- Microsoft Learn (https://docs.microsoft.com/en-us/learn): Provides free online courses and learning paths for various Microsoft technologies and IT concepts.

- Google's IT Support Professional Certificate (https://grow.google/programs/it-support): A beginner-friendly program that covers IT fundamentals, networking, and security concepts.

- Udemy (https://www.udemy.com): Offers a wide variety of IT courses taught by industry professionals, including computer basics, programming, and web development.

- "Computers For Dummies" by Dan Gookin: A beginner-friendly book that introduces basic computer concepts and terminology.

- YouTube Channels (e.g., Computerphile, TechGumbo, Linus Tech Tips): Offer free video tutorials on various IT topics, from computer hardware to software and programming concepts.

If you're serious about learning, I'd recommend CompTIA A+Core 1 and Core2: https://www.comptia.org/certifications/a

CompTIA A+ 220-1101 (Core 1) domains:

1. Mobile Devices
   - Laptop hardware and components
   - Mobile device hardware and components
   - Mobile device setup and configuration
2. Networking
   - Networking hardware devices
   - Network components and their functions
   - Network configuration concepts
   - Network troubleshooting
3. Hardware
   - PC hardware and components
   - Peripherals and device connectivity
   - Storage devices and media
   - Hardware troubleshooting
4. Virtualization and Cloud Computing
   - Virtualization technologies
   - Cloud computing models and concepts
   - Cloud services and their features
5. Hardware and Network Troubleshooting
   - Troubleshooting methodologies
   - Hardware and device troubleshooting
   - Network troubleshooting
   - Troubleshooting tools and resources

CompTIA A+ 220-1102 (Core 2) domains:

1. Operating Systems
   - Windows operating systems
   - macOS operating systems
   - Linux operating systems

- Operating system installation and upgrade processes
- Operating system management tools and features

2. Security
   - Physical security measures
   - Logical security concepts
   - Wireless and wired network security
   - User account and access control management
   - Security best practices and policies

3. Software Troubleshooting
   - Troubleshooting PC and mobile operating systems
   - Troubleshooting software applications
   - Troubleshooting malware and security issues
   - Troubleshooting tools and resources for software issues

4. Operational Procedures
   - IT documentation and processes
   - IT professional communication and collaboration
   - Disaster prevention and recovery
   - Best practices for environmental and safety concerns
   - Compliance with laws and regulations

Even if you're starting from scratch, the information in this book will still be helpful, and by the end, you'll know some of the best security practices.

CHAPTER 1

SECURITY OBJECTIVES & BEST PRACTICES

> "No technology that's connected to the Internet is unhackable."
>
> Abhijit Naskar

One concept will help you understand the root of all cybersecurity. It is one concept to rule them all, the security objectives.

Security objectives are the goals or outcomes an organization wants to achieve to ensure the confidentiality, integrity, and availability of its data and information systems. These three components, also known as the CIA triad, are the foundation of any cybersecurity program.

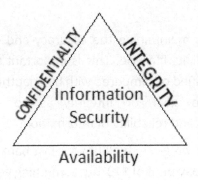

CONFIDENTIALITY:

Confidentiality pertains to safeguarding sensitive information from unauthorized access or disclosure. This can include any data that an organization considers sensitive, such as personal information, financial data, trade secrets, and proprietary information. The goal of confidentiality is to ensure that only authorized individuals or systems can access the information. This is typically achieved using access controls such as passwords, biometric authentication, or encryption.

An example of confidentiality is if a government wanted to make its knowledge of extraterrestrial technology Top Secret! That information is confidential whether the information was on a server somewhere in the nation's capital or typed on a document from 1947 locked in a vault. Please note, I mention UFOs in some of my books, but I promise you I don't have any exposure to this information... or do I? Even if I did, I would not tell you because it's confidential, and I am not trying to get "Snowdened."

INTEGRITY:

Integrity means maintaining the accuracy and consistency of data throughout its lifecycle. This is important to ensure that data is not modified or tampered with by unauthorized users or processes. The goal of integrity is to maintain the trustworthiness and reliability of information.

For information integrity, think of your last bank transaction. If you make a bill payment of $10, but something goes wrong, and a few "0's" are added to the transaction, this would breach the data's integrity. Solid data integrity means that the original state of the data is not altered as it is processed, stored, or transferred.

AVAILABILITY:

Availability means the information and systems are accessible to authorized users when needed. This can include preventing downtime due to technical failures, natural disasters, or cyber-attacks. Availability aims to ensure that critical systems and data are always able to be reached. Redundancy, disaster recovery plans, and business continuity measures help make availability possible. Redundancy involves having backup systems or equipment that can take over in case of failure. Disaster recovery plans provide a roadmap for restoring critical systems and data in case of a significant outage or disaster. Business continuity measures involve planning how the organization will continue operating in case of an unexpected interruption or disaster.

Whenever significant sites, such as Google, Facebook, or your mom's website, goes down, this is a loss of availability. An organization can lose money, credibility, or even human life if the business or mission system depends on being accessible.

Assets

Not everything in your house needs the same level of protection. If a burglar broke in, stole your video games, and tossed some things around, you would be upset. But if someone broke in and took seven thousand dollars worth of jewelry and your KIA Forte that you need to get to work, this is a real problem. This is a loss that will take you some time to recover from.

In the same way, organizations have information and systems with different levels of importance. Computers with a high level of value are called "assets." These can be endpoint devices like laptops and desktops, mobile devices like smartphones, or high-level systems on which everyone shares the resources, like servers. The organization has to protect the confidentiality, integrity, and availability of the information on the assets.

To protect this information, the organization uses security controls. Security controls can be physical, technical, operational, and even environmental. These controls are so important some entire careers and industries rely on them. Once you know these best practices, you will recognize them across multiple industries, from the government to aerospace, healthcare, and retail.

Each control applies to all aspects of security protection and can be associated with protecting users, data, networks, devices, applications, buildings, support systems, processes, and other parts of an organization.

Security Frameworks Referenced for Security Objectives

All security standards and frameworks have a list of security controls or security best practices that you can reference to get deeper into the weeds of protecting organization systems. Here are a few references:

- NIST Special Publication 800-53

- ISO/IEC 27001

- CIS Critical Security Controls

- NIST Cybersecurity Framework

- Payment Card Industry Data Security Standard (PCI DSS)

- Health Insurance Portability and Accountability Act (HIPAA) Security Rule

- Federal Risk and Authorization Management Program (FedRAMP)

- HITRUST Common Security Framework (CSF)

- Control Objectives for Information and Related Technologies (COBIT)

- Cloud Security Alliance (CSA) Cloud Controls Matrix (CCM)

Basic IT Security Training & Resources

Here are some resources you can use to learn the basics of IT security and compliance:

- Cybrary: Offers free and paid online cybersecurity courses covering a wide range of topics from beginner to advanced.(https://www.cybrary.it/)

- SANS Cyber Aces: Provides free online courses on cybersecurity fundamentals, including networking, operating systems, and system administration. (https://www.cyberaces.org/)

- Coursera: Features a variety of IT security courses, including beginner-friendly options, taught by experts from top universities. (https://www.coursera.org/browse/information-technology/security)

- edX: Offers a range of cybersecurity courses from universities and institutions worldwide, including introductory courses on IT security. (https://www.edx.org/learn/cybersecurity)

- Google's IT Support Professional Certificate: Covers various IT support topics, including an introduction to IT security. (https://grow.google/programs/it-support)

- Khan Academy: Provides free online courses on various subjects, including a course on internet security and privacy.

- Udemy: Offers various IT shecurity courses, ranging from beginner to advanced levels. (https://www.udemy.com/topic/it-security/)

- **Infosec Skills**: Offers a free trial to access their cybersecurity training platform, including beginner-friendly IT security courses. (https://www.infosecinstitute.com/skills/)

- YouTube Channels: Several channels offer free video tutorials on IT security topics, such as NetworkChuck, Professor Messer, and Eli the Computer Guy. [NetworkChuck on Youtube](https://www.youtube.com/c/NetworkChuck), [Professor Messer on Youtube](https://www.youtube.com/user/professormesser) [Eli the Computer Guy on Youtube](https://www.youtube.com/user/elithecomputerguy)

- **LinkedIn Learning** (formerly Lynda.com): Offers a wide range of IT security courses, from beginner to advanced levels, with a free trial available (https://www.linkedin.com/learning/topics/it-security)

To download the spreadsheet of best practice and security control spreadsheets:
http://convocourses.com/courses/bestsecuritypractices

CHAPTER 2

IDENTIFY AND PROTECT
THE BASELINE

"Know the enemy and know yourself; in a hundred battles, you will never be in peril. When you are ignorant of the enemy, but know yourself, your chances of winning or losing are equal. If ignorant both of your enemy and yourself, you are certain in every battle to be in peril."

~Sun Tzu, The Art of War

For an organization, knowing the baseline is like the organization knowing itself. The "baseline" is knowing, tracking, and documenting the 35 Windows XYZ Dell laptops installed with Adobe Acrobat Version X and New Browse Version X at Nevada site 51 in a small office network. And any variation away from that is outside of the established baseline. If there are any changes, fluctuations, or updates, we need to know about them and track those changes.

Identifying and protecting the baseline is a concept that is important in cybersecurity. It means you need to identify what is normal regarding computer activity. That way, when something is different, you notice and take action. This action might include putting measures in place to protect it from malicious activity.

For organizations, there needs to be a process that tracks changes to the baseline, sometimes known as configuration management or change control. It is an important concept that you will see in most organizations.

By identifying and protecting the baseline, you can help to keep your computer and personal information safe from hackers and other online threats.

System Baseline

As a cybersecurity expert, one essential practice strongly recommended for securing your computer system is creating a system baseline.

A system baseline refers to the snapshot of the configuration and settings of your computer system at a particular point in time. It records the state of your system's hardware, software, and network configurations, including operating system versions, drivers, and software installed.

Why is it important to have a system baseline?

A system baseline is a reference point for understanding your computer system's current state and detecting any changes or anomalies that may indicate security threats. It helps identify and address security vulnerabilities, malware infections, or system failures, preventing potential attacks or data breaches.

By maintaining a system baseline, you can monitor your system's changes, easily detect deviations from its standard configuration, and address them promptly before they can cause harm.

Here's a list of solutions to inventory and track hardware assets:

1. **Automated Asset Discovery Tools**: Use tools like Lansweeper, SolarWinds Network Performance Monitor, or Spiceworks to discover, inventory, and track hardware assets connected to the organization's network.

2. **Centralized Asset Management System**: Implement a centralized asset management system, such as ServiceNow, Jira Service Management, or BMC Remedy, to maintain an up-to-date inventory of all hardware assets.

3. **Network Access Control (NAC)**: Implement a NAC solution like Cisco ISE, Aruba ClearPass, or ForeScout CounterACT to control access to the network based on

the asset's compliance with the organization's security policies.

4. **Barcode or QR Code System**: Label all hardware assets with barcodes or QR codes and use a scanning solution, such as Wasp Barcode or Asset Panda, to track and manage the inventory.

5. **Radio Frequency Identification (RFID)**: Use RFID tags and a suitable tracking system to identify and track hardware assets in real-time automatically.

6. **Mobile Device Management (MDM)**: Employ an MDM solution like Microsoft Intune, VMware Workspace ONE, or Jamf Pro to manage and track mobile devices, such as smartphones and tablets, that access the organization's network.

7. **Periodic Asset Audits**: Conduct regular physical and network-based audits to verify the accuracy of the hardware inventory and detect unauthorized assets.

8. **Asset Lifecycle Management**: Establish a process for managing hardware assets throughout their lifecycle, from procurement to disposal, to ensure accurate inventory and proper decommissioning.

9. **Access Controls and Role-Based Privileges**: Implement access controls and role-based privileges to restrict who can add, modify, or remove hardware assets from the inventory.

Inventory and Control of Software Assets:

Establishing a baseline must include the software. The organization will list all the software with each version of the system installed. This inventory can be tied to a whitelist (list of approved applications – excluding everything else) or a blacklist (list of restricted apps). At the last organization I worked for, they controlled the software by making it so no one could download or install anything without approval. You had to request software that was not on their approved list, and some software had only a limited number of licenses, so only a few people were authorized to use it.

If the organization does not know its software versions, they will lose track of the applications and have instances that are old and unsupported. This is known as end of life (EOL) or end of support (EOS).

All vendors, from Adobe to WinZip, have an end-of-support date for their software versions. End of support means that if the software breaks, they cannot help fix it. Or, more likely, malicious hackers find and exploit new weaknesses in old software.

1. **IT Asset Management (ITAM) Tools:** Leverage ITAM tools such as ServiceNow, Lansweeper, or ManageEngine AssetExplorer to discover, track, and manage software assets across the organization.

2. **Software Inventory Tools:** Use specialized software inventory tools like SCCM (System Center Configuration Manager), PDQ Inventory, or Snipe-IT to maintain an up-to-date inventory of software installations and licenses.

3. **Software Asset Management (SAM) Tools:** Implement SAM tools like Flexera, Snow Software, or 1E to manage software licenses, ensure compliance, and optimize software spend.

4. **Open Source Tools:** Utilize open source solutions like OCS Inventory NG, GLPI, or Spiceworks to inventory and track software assets.

5. **Network Scanners:** Employ network scanners such as Nmap or OpenVAS to discover software assets on the network and maintain an accurate inventory.

6. **Vulnerability Scanners:** Leverage vulnerability scanners like Qualys, Tenable Nessus, or Rapid7 Nexpose to identify and track software assets with known vulnerabilities.

7. **Cloud Asset Management:** Utilize cloud-specific tools like AWS Config, Google Cloud Asset Inventory, or Microsoft Azure Asset Inventory to monitor and manage software assets in cloud environments.

8. **Container and Virtualization Management:** Implement solutions like Kubernetes, Docker, or VMware vCenter to track and manage software assets in containerized and virtualized environments.

9. **Configuration Management Tools:** Leverage configuration management tools like Ansible, Puppet, or Chef to maintain an accurate inventory of software assets and enforce a desired configuration state.

10. **SIEM and Log Management:** Utilize Security Information and Event Management (SIEM) tools like Splunk, LogRhythm, or IBM QRadar to collect, analyze,

and correlate log data from various sources to track software assets and detect anomalies.

To implement a baseline, companies must have technical and procedural measures. They can use specialized tools to scan their network for devices and collect data on their assets. This data must be kept updated because assets can come and go, making inventory a dynamic process. To ensure that only authorized software runs on your company's devices, different techniques and tools are available for managing your software.

Secure Configuration (AKA System Hardening)

A list of software and hardware is just one part of a baseline. All software and hardware need to have a secure configuration. This is known as system hardening because it makes the system difficult to hack. Think of it in terms of criminals choosing a target. When possible, criminals choose "soft targets." They want an easy score. It's much easier to burglarize someone's house with no security than a military base with armed guards and 7-foot barbed fences.

So you want to make your system a hard target.

System hardening includes creating accounts for different roles on each system and limiting the rights for access to installation and modifications to only privileged users. Other examples would be, restricting connections, updating the patches, turning on the event logs, and applying all restrictions needed to match the organization's policy. And you would do this on all systems. The secure configuration will vary from system to system and depends on the organization's needs.

This is important because when a company gets new equipment or software, it's usually set up to be easy to use, with a default setting. Unfortunately, hackers can exploit weaknesses in the default settings, like easy-to-guess passwords, old protocols, and unnecessary software that can be exploited.

That's why setting up new equipment and software with strong security settings is important.

Security settings alone are not enough. You also need to keep those settings up to date, even as new vulnerabilities are discovered and new software is added, aka, configuration management.

Some tools and procedures can help with configuration management. For example, there are publicly available security baselines that companies can use as a starting point. Companies can also create their security configuration script to set up security settings to protect their data. Then they can apply operating system and security patches, install application software, and run a security quality assurance test.

It's also important to document deviations from the standard settings and use configuration management tools to ensure that all equipment and software are set up properly.

Suppose you are a security manager at a medium-sized company that provides cloud-based services to various clients. You are responsible for ensuring that your company's assets and software are configured securely and comply with industry standards and best practices.

The goal is to establish and maintain secure configurations for all enterprise assets and software, including servers, workstations, network devices, mobile devices, cloud services, applications, databases, and more.

There are tools to help secure each type of system, such as the CIS Benchmark. The CIS Benchmarks are consensus-based configuration guidelines for various technologies developed by a community of experts and validated by independent auditors. There is also a tool from the Department of Defense called security technical implementation guides (STIGS). These tools provide detailed recommendations for settings, parameters, options, and values that can enhance the security posture of your systems.

Once the security configuration is created, you must apply the baselines to all your assets and software and ensure they are enforced and maintained throughout their lifecycle. You can use various tools and methods to automate this process, such as configuration management software, scripts, policies, procedures, checklists, etc.

You must monitor and audit your assets and software for any deviations from the secure configuration baselines. You can use tools such as scanners, agents, logs, alerts, reports, etc., to detect and report any unauthorized or unexpected changes in your systems. You must also review and analyze the audit results and take corrective actions if needed.

For more details, check out:
http://convocourses.com/courses/bestsecuritypractice

Reference to Baseline Best Practices

The NIST 800 covers baseline configurations in the "CM" family of security controls. There is another group of controls called "CIS Critical Security Controls." These are used by organizations worldwide, including governments and large corporations. CIS Critical Security Controls address the baseline in CIS Controls 1 & 2, covering the inventory and control of hardware and software assets. CIS Control 3 covers secure configurations.

CIS 1, Hardware Baseline

CIS Control 1 addresses the physical components of computers. I recently got a job with the government; they issued me a computer. They tracked it with an "asset tag" or serial number, had me sign a document taking ownership of the computer, and put all of my information with the system name and serial number into an online database. Even though I take the computer home and work from a home office, they always know where it is. The organization also tracked the accessories that go with the hardware. They know where all hardware is located, the status of it, and who has it, along with peripheral devices. They have a process to deal with lost or stolen equipment. And when it is time to decommission or transfer the system to another site or user, they have a process that will continue to track it.

When organizations don't have a good hardware baseline, I have seen users just plug random devices into the network. I have seen gaming servers, music servers, personal laptops; you name it, added to an organizations network with no approval or tracking. It's important to know what hardware is on your network and where it is.

CIS 2, Software Baseline, and NIST CM

CIS Control 2, Inventory and Control of Software Assets is focused on identifying and tracking all of the software across the network. The government standard also has a control that addresses this. The challenge of tracking software is that it is so easy to download and install on systems. Each computer can have dozens of instances of software. I have been in organizations where this is tracked manually. It sucks. And it is not effective. The best way is to automate the process and lockdown the systems so that regular users cannot just download and install whatever they want.

Baseline Security Training & Resources

You can download tools and procedures in a few places to help set up secure baselines. Most vendors (i.e., Microsoft, Oracle, Cisco) offer lots of instructions to help configure their devices. But here are some more resources:

- DISA STIGs (Security Technical Implementation Guides): Offers a collection of security guidelines for various technologies developed by the Defense Information Systems Agency (DISA). [DISA STIGs] (https://public.cyber.mil/stigs/downloads/)

- CIS Benchmarks: Developed by the Center for Internet Security (CIS), these benchmarks provide a set of best practices for securely configuring various technologies. [CIS Benchmarks] (https://www.cisecurity.org/cis-benchmarks/)

- NIST National Checklist Program Repository: A collection of security checklists, baselines, and guidelines for various IT products provided by the National Institute of Standards and Technology (NIST). [NIST Checklists] (https://nvd.nist.gov/ncp/repository)

- Microsoft Security Baselines: Offers a set of recommended security settings for various Microsoft products, including Windows, Office, and Azure. [Microsoft Security Baselines] (https://docs.microsoft.com/en-us/windows/security/threat-protection/windows-security-baselines)

- VMware Security Hardening Guides: Provides guidelines for securely configuring VMware products, such as vSphere and NSX. [VMware Security Hardening Guides] (https://www.vmware.com/security/hardening-guides.html)

- Amazon Web Services (AWS) Well-Architected Framework: Offers a set of best practices and guidelines for building secure and efficient AWS infrastructure. [AWS Well-Architected Framework] (https://aws.amazon.com/architecture/well-architected/)

- Azure Security Benchmark: Provides security best practices for Microsoft Azure customers to secure their cloud resources. [Azure Security Benchmark] (https://docs.microsoft.com/en-us/azure/security/benchmark/)

- Google Cloud Security Command Center: Offers a suite of tools and guidelines for Google Cloud Platform customers to secure their cloud resources. [Google

Cloud Security Command Center]
(https://cloud.google.com/security-command-center)

- Red Hat Security Guide: Provides security guidelines and best practices for Red Hat Enterprise Linux (RHEL) systems. [Red Hat Security Guide] (https://access.redhat.com/documentation/en-us/red_hat_enterprise_linux/8/html/security_hardening/index)

- Apple macOS Security Configuration Guides: Offers a set of guidelines for securely configuring macOS systems in enterprise environments. [macOS Security Configuration Guides] (https://www.apple.com/business/docs/resources/)

CHAPTER 3

ACCESS CONTROL

Username : admin
Password : admin

admin:password

"Passwords are like underwear. Don't let people see it, change it very often, and you shouldn't share it with strangers."

~Chris Pirillo

I n this chapter, we will discuss account and access management.

Account and Access Management are closely related concepts in information security, often used interchangeably. Both aim to ensure the appropriate level of access control for users within an organization by regulating their access to sensitive data and system resources. While they are distinct concepts, there are several similarities between them:

- Authentication: Both account and access management involve verifying the identity of a user attempting to access a system or resource. This is usually done through a combination of credentials, such as usernames and passwords, or other authentication methods like biometrics or two-factor authentication.

- Authorization: Both processes involve determining what a user is allowed to do once their identity is verified. This includes defining the specific resources they can access and their actions on those resources (e.g., read, write, delete, or modify).

- Principle of Least Privilege: Both account and access management are guided by the principle of least privilege, which states that users should only have the minimum access necessary to perform their job functions. This helps to reduce the potential for unauthorized access or misuse of sensitive data.

- User Lifecycle Management: Both concepts involve the management of user accounts throughout their lifecycle, from creation to deactivation. This includes onboarding new users, updating access permissions as needed, and revoking access when a user leaves the organization or changes roles.

- Audit and Compliance: Account and access management must maintain user access and activity records for auditing and compliance purposes. This helps organizations demonstrate adherence to regulatory requirements and identify potential issues or security risks.

- Integration with Security Systems: Account and access management are often integrated with other security systems within an organization, such as firewalls, intrusion detection systems, and security information and event management (SIEM) tools. This integration helps to enhance overall security and visibility across the organization.

Both account and access management are essential in mitigating security risks within an organization. Confidentiality, integrity, and availability are protected by controlling user access to sensitive data and resources, focusing on authentication, authorization, least privilege, user lifecycle management, audit and compliance, and integration with other security systems.

Account Management

Whenever you get a new IT job, one of the first things they do is create an account that allows you access to the needed work. They have to create, modify, maintain, and remove all accounts in the organization. How do they manage this?

In cybersecurity, "account management" refers to managing user accounts and access rights to ensure the security and integrity of an organization's systems and data. It is a critical aspect of cybersecurity that involves creating, maintaining, and deactivating user accounts, assigning access privileges and permissions, enforcing security policies and standards, and monitoring user activity.

At a conceptual level, account management is about controlling access to sensitive information and resources. It involves implementing robust security measures to prevent unauthorized access, managing user accounts and access privileges, enforcing security policies and standards, and monitoring user activity to detect and prevent cyber threats.

Account management ensures only authorized personnel can access specific resources and data within an organization.

Steps of Account Management

By following these steps, organizations can minimize the risk of cyber threats and protect their sensitive information and assets.

Creating User Accounts:

This involves creating user accounts for authorized personnel who need access to the organization's systems and data. User accounts can be created using various methods, including manual creation and automated account provisioning.

Manual account creation involves using forms, templates, or other tools to ensure user accounts are created consistently and with the necessary security controls.

Automated account provisioning involves using software tools to automate the creation of user accounts. This approach can streamline creating user accounts and reduce the risk of errors or inconsistencies.

Ensure user accounts are created with the necessary security controls. This includes using strong passwords that meet certain complexity requirements, such as length, use of special characters, and requiring users to change their passwords periodically. Multi-factor authentication can also provide an additional layer of security, such as requiring users to provide a password and a one-time code generated by an app or hardware device.

Maintaining User Accounts:

Maintaining user accounts involves disabling or deleting inactive accounts. Inactive accounts can pose a security risk, as they may still have access to digital resources even if the user is no longer employed or authorized to access them. Therefore, organizations should establish procedures for disabling or deleting inactive accounts and periodically review their user account database to identify and remove inactive accounts.

Assigning Access Privileges and Permissions:

Assigning privileges involves determining the level of access that each user is granted based on their job roles and responsibilities. In addition, access privileges should be granted on a need-to-know basis to prevent unauthorized access to sensitive information.

Organizations should establish a process for assigning access privileges and permissions to ensure that access privileges are granted appropriately.

Enforcing Security Policies and Standards:

Security policies and standards are established to provide a framework for ensuring digital resources' confidentiality, integrity, and availability. This involves defining rules and procedures for controlling resource access and handling security incidents.

These policies define the level of access that users should have to digital resources based on their job responsibilities and security clearance levels. User access policies should be regularly reviewed and updated to ensure that they are aligned with current business requirements and security threats.

Monitoring User Activity:

This involves tracking and analyzing the actions of users with access to sensitive information or systems to detect any suspicious or unauthorized activity. By monitoring user activity, organizations can quickly identify potential security breaches and take prompt action to prevent further damage.

Organizations should establish clear logging and monitoring policies and procedures to monitor user activity effectively. This includes setting up systems to collect and store user activity logs and implementing tools and processes to analyze these logs for signs of suspicious activity.

Examples of user activity that may be monitored include failed login attempts, successful logins, changes to user accounts, file access and modification, and system configuration changes.

Access Management

Access management in cybersecurity involves controlling and managing resource access based on a user's privileges and permissions. The primary objective of access management is to grant access only to authorized individuals while keeping unauthorized users from gaining access.

Access management can be achieved through various means, such as authentication, authorization, and access control mechanisms. These mechanisms help to enforce security policies and standards, limit the scope of access permissions, and protect against cyber threats.

Authentication is the process of verifying the identity of a user before granting access to a resource. This can be achieved through various means, such as passwords, biometrics, smart cards, and tokens. Once the user is authenticated, authorization determines what actions the user is allowed to perform. Authorization can be granted based on job roles, security clearance levels, and need-to-know basis.

Access control mechanisms, such as firewalls, intrusion detection systems, and access control systems, can also be used to enforce security policies and limit access to resources. Firewalls can prevent unauthorized access to a network by filtering traffic based on predefined rules. Intrusion detection systems can detect and prevent attacks by monitoring network traffic for suspicious activity. Access control systems can limit resource access based on user privileges and permissions and provide audit trails for monitoring user activity.

Security Framework Reference to Access and Account Controls

Access & account controls are covered in the NIST 800-53 under the AC Access Control family. CIS Control 5 is Account Management, and CIS Control 6 is Access Control Management. Each has a breakdown of multiple safeguards an organization can use to secure its environment.

Access and Account Control Training & Resources

Access & account controls are a big part of cybersecurity. There is a lot of great training on this topic:

- Coursera - Access Controls: A course provided by the University of Colorado that covers the basics of access control and identity management. [Access Controls Course](https://www.coursera.org/learn/access-controls)

- Cybrary - Identity and Access Management (IAM) Training: Offers a free online course that covers the fundamentals of IAM, including access control and account management. [IAM Training](https://www.cybrary.it/course/identity-access-management-iam/)

- Udemy - Access Control and Identity Management: A course that explores access control, authentication, authorization, and identity management concepts. [Access Control and Identity Management]

(https://www.udemy.com/course/access-control-and-identity-management/)

- Pluralsight - Access Control Techniques: A course that covers various access control techniques, models, and best practices. [Access Control Techniques] (https://www.pluralsight.com/courses/access-control-techniques)

- LinkedIn Learning - Access Control Foundations: Offers a course that explores the basics of access control, including authentication, authorization, and identity management. [Access Control Foundations] (https://www.linkedin.com/learning/access-control-foundations)

- SANS - Access Control Security Training: SANS offers several courses on access control and identity management as part of their security training offerings. [SANS Training] (https://www.sans.org/courses/)

- Microsoft Learn - Implementing Access Control: Provides a learning path that covers access control and identity management concepts in the context of Microsoft Azure. [Implementing Access Control] (https://docs.microsoft.com/en-us/learn/paths/implement-access-control/)

- Amazon Web Services (AWS) Training - Identity and Access Management: Offers a variety of resources and training materials related to AWS Identity and Access Management (IAM) services. [AWS IAM Training] (https://aws.amazon.com/iam/getting-started/)

- Google Cloud Training - Access Control and Security: Provides training resources covering access control and best practices for Google Cloud Platform services. [Google Cloud Access Control and Security] (https://cloud.google.com/security/getting-started)

- Infosec Institute - Access Control and Identity Management: An online training program covers access control and identity management concepts, including account management best practices. [Infosec Access Control and Identity Management] (https://www.infosecinstitute.com/courses/access-control-and-identity-management/)

CHAPTER 4

CONTINUOUS MONITORING AND LOGS

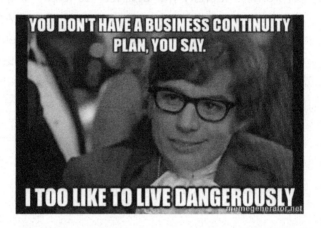

YOU DON'T HAVE A BUSINESS CONTINUITY PLAN, YOU SAY.

I TOO LIKE TO LIVE DANGEROUSLY

> "If you spend more on coffee than on IT security, you will be hacked. What's more, you deserve to be hacked."
>
> ~Richard Clarke

I can summarize this entire chapter for you: Computer logs are very important. They are the eyes and ears of the network. They must be collected and watched constantly.

Continuous Monitoring, also called ConMon or Continuous Control Monitoring (CCM), is a method utilized by security and operations analysts to oversee the well-being of infrastructure, such as networks and cloud-based applications.

IT businesses use the technology and methodology of continuous Monitoring to enable quick identification of security and compliance threats within the infrastructure.

Continuous Monitoring provides organizations with real-time data from public and hybrid cloud environments and supports crucial security processes like threat intelligence, forensics, root cause analysis, and incident response.

The data sources typically monitored include system logs, network traffic, user behavior, vulnerability scans, and threat intelligence feeds.

Vulnerability Management

Vulnerability management is the biggest part of the continuous monitoring pie, particularly in large organizations with numerous assets. As the number of assets increases, the need for continuous management of potential vulnerabilities also grows. It is not uncommon for networks to have thousands of vulnerabilities. In more than one environment I was in, we had hundreds of thousands of vulnerabilities.

Every application, firmware, and operating system may contain vulnerabilities. As software is constantly updated or extended, each change introduces the risk of new weaknesses that attackers can exploit. Therefore, developing a comprehensive plan to continuously assess and track vulnerabilities across all enterprise assets within an organization's infrastructure is essential. This plan aims to remediate vulnerabilities and minimize the window of opportunity for attackers.

Organizations should monitor public and private industry sources for new threats and vulnerability information. A documented vulnerability management process should be established and maintained for all enterprise assets. This documentation should be reviewed and updated annually, or when significant enterprise changes occur, that could impact this safeguard.

A risk-based remediation strategy should be established and documented in a remediation process, with reviews conducted monthly or more frequently. Operating system and application updates should be performed monthly or more frequently on enterprise assets through automated patch management. What organizations will usually do, is create a security policy that says something like "critical" vulnerabilities must be fixed within 7 days and "Low" vulnerabilities must be patched within 30 days, or something like that, where the speed of remediation is based on the potential risk.

Automated vulnerability scans of internal enterprise assets should be conducted quarterly or more frequently. The organization can use a special tool that follows a standard called Security Content Automation Protocol (SCAP) to do scans. SCAP helps you find and fix problems faster. They should scan systems inside the network at least four times a year or more often if they can. There are two main types of scans: one where the tool logs in to the device (authenticated, aka credentialed) and one where it doesn't (unauthenticated or non-credentialed).

Last but not least, organizations must remediate detected vulnerabilities in software through established processes and tooling monthly or more frequently, based on the remediation process. Organizations can proactively manage vulnerabilities and enhance their overall security posture by implementing these measures.

Audit Logs

Logs (aka event logs, audit logs, or log files) are text notifications that give the status of a system. It's a record of what is going on at any given moment. All devices have logs. They are necessary for fixing computers, configuring software, and monitoring security. Since many logs can be created, log management is necessary. Log management ensures that the organization only records important data. It must be stored, protected and remain accessible to those who need it. Firewalls, proxies, VPNs, and remote access systems are just a few examples of software and hardware resources that should be used to save important data.

Additionally, best practices encourage businesses to scan their logs regularly and compare them to their inventory of IT assets to determine whether each asset is indeed connected to your network and producing logs.

One aspect of efficient log management commonly disregarded is the requirement to have all systems time-synchronized to a single Network Time Protocol (NTP) server to construct a precise sequence of events.

During system implementation, two distinct log types are configured independently:

- *System logs offer information on system-level events, such as the process's beginning and end timings.*

- *Audit logs include user-level events such as logins and file access. Audit logs are critical for investigating cybersecurity incidents and require more configuration effort than system logs.*

More about Audit Logs then you want to know

Logs contain information about user activities, system events, and other security-related data that can help detect potential security threats and vulnerabilities. An audit log is a complete record of all actions taken on a system. It is useful for investigating security incidents, analyzing system performance, and ensuring compliance with regulations and policies. The log provides a trail of evidence that can answer questions such as "who did what, when, and from where?" without any confusion. Examples of events that may be logged include user logins and logouts, system errors, file access, changes to system settings, and security-related incidents like failed login attempts or unauthorized access attempts. Each event in the audit log typically includes the following information:

- **Date and time**: *when the event occurred*
- **User:** *The identity of the user who performed the activity*
- **Source:** *The location or system where the activity occurred*
- **Action:** *The specific activity that was performed*
- **Result:** *The outcome of the activity (e.g., success or failure)*
- **Additional details:** *Other relevant information about the event, such as IP addresses, file names, or error codes*

Logs are usually kept securely and may even be encrypted for added protection. Only authorized personnel should have access to it. Regular reviews of the audit trails are necessary to identify security threats and opportunities for improvement.

Advantages of having audit logs

Audit logs offer several advantages to organizations, including:

- **Enhanced security:** Audit logs keep a detailed record of all activities performed on a system, which helps organizations quickly and effectively identify and respond to potential security threats and vulnerabilities.

- **Compliance:** Many regulations and standards require organizations to maintain audit logs, such as Health Insurance Portability and Accountability Act (HIPAA), Payment Card Industry Data Security Standard (PCI-DSS), and Sarbanes-Oxley Act (SOX). Organizations can avoid costly fines and legal penalties by complying with these regulations.

- **Forensic analysis:** Audit logs can be used during a security incident. By analyzing the logs, organizations can determine the cause of the incident and take appropriate measures to prevent it from happening again.

- **Performance analysis:** Audit logs can also be used to analyze the performance of systems and applications. This can help identify areas where improvements can be made to enhance system performance and security.

- **Accountability:** Audit logs provide a record of user activity on a system, which promotes accountability among users. This can discourage users from engaging in malicious or unauthorized activities, as they know their actions are being recorded and can be traced back to them.

- **Root cause analysis:** Audit logs can be used to perform root cause analysis, which helps identify the underlying cause of system issues or errors. This can help organizations resolve issues more quickly and effectively.

- **Improving business processes:** Audit logs can provide insights into business processes' performance. This can help organizations identify inefficiencies or bottlenecks in their processes and take steps to improve them.

- **Risk management:** Organizations can use audit logs to detect possible security threats and take preventive actions to minimize them. This, in turn, can lower the chances of security breaches and the consequent expenses and harm to reputation.

Organizations can ensure a comprehensive and efficient audit log management process by selecting an auditing solution that covers the most assets in the least time. This can help improve security, compliance, and overall IT operations.

Security Framework Reference to Logs and Continuous Monitoring

The NIST 800 has the family AU, Audit and Accountability, that addresses the need for an organization to enable logs. The security control family CA covers the need for continuous monitoring. CIS Control 7, Continuous Vulnerability Management, CIS Control 8, Audit Controls Management and CIS Control 13, Network Monitoring and Defense are the three main safeguards of continuous monitoring. We will cover CIS 13 in the network chapter.

The NIST has a document for continuous monitoring called NIST SP 800-137, Information Security Continous Monitoring (ISCM) for Federal Information systems and Organizations.

Continuous Monitoring, Auditing Training & Resources

Here are some training resources for continuous monitoring and audit logs:

- Coursera - Continuous Monitoring and Security Operations: The University of Colorado provides a course covering continuous monitoring, security operations, and log management. (https://www.coursera.org/learn/continuous-monitoring-security-operations)

- Udemy - Log Analysis and Continuous Monitoring: A course that explores log analysis techniques and continuous monitoring strategies for various IT environments. (https://www.udemy.com/course/log-analysis-and-continuous-monitoring/)

- Pluralsight - Monitoring and Auditing Course covers various monitoring and auditing techniques, including log analysis and continuous monitoring. (https://www.pluralsight.com/courses/monitoring-auditing)

- Cybrary - Continuous Monitoring and Security Operations: A free online course that covers the fundamentals of continuous monitoring, security operations, and log management. (https://www.cybrary.it/course/continuous-monitoring-security-operations/)

- SANS - Continuous Monitoring Training: SANS offers continuous monitoring, log analysis, and security operations courses. (https://www.sans.org/courses/)

- LinkedIn Learning - Log Monitoring and Analysis: Offers a course that explores the basics of log monitoring, analysis, and continuous monitoring. (https://www.linkedin.com/learning/log-monitoring-and-analysis)

- Microsoft Learn - Monitoring and Auditing in Azure: Provides a learning path that covers monitoring and auditing concepts in the context of Microsoft Azure. (https://docs.microsoft.com/en-us/learn/paths/azure-monitoring-auditing/)

- Amazon Web Services (AWS) Training - Monitoring, Logging, and Performance: Offers a variety of resources and training materials related to AWS monitoring, logging, and performance optimization. (https://aws.amazon.com/training/learn-about/monitoring-logging-performance/)

- Google Cloud Training - Monitoring, Logging, and Debugging: Provides training resources that cover monitoring, logging, and debugging best practices for Google Cloud Platform services. [Google Cloud Monitoring, Logging, and Debugging](https://cloud.google.com/training/courses/monitoring-logging-debugging)

- Infosec Institute - Auditing and Monitoring: An online training program that covers auditing and monitoring concepts, including log analysis and continuous monitoring. (https://www.infosecinstitute.com/courses/auditing-and-monitoring/)

CHAPTER 5

EMAIL, BROWSERS & MALWARE

> "Trying to secure the internet without addressing the underlying problem of malicious software is like trying to secure an ocean by putting a band-aid on a shark."
>
> ~Jonathan Zdziarski,
> A cybersecurity expert and author.

Two of the most common places that malicious hackers hit (attack vectors) are emails and browsers. They usually use malicious software, malware, to do this.

Think about it, how many suspicious emails are sent to spam, and how many scam sites have you gone to versus someone hacking into your computer to take over your screen?

Let's discuss how some attacks use email and browsers as attack vectors.

EMAIL ATTACKS:

Email is a primary communication channel, and cybercriminals exploit it by sending malicious emails to unsuspecting users. These emails typically contain links or attachments that, when clicked or downloaded, install malware on the user's computer. If the computer does not have a secure configuration, that's when the organization is screwed.

Some common types of email attacks include:

- **Phishing:** This method of cybercrime involves the creation of emails that resemble those from reputable sources, like banks or social media sites. The intent is to deceive users into providing their login credentials or other confidential data.

- **Spear-phishing:** This is a more targeted form of phishing, where cybercriminals research their victims and create customized emails that are more convincing.

- **Malware attachments:** These are emails that contain attachments that, when opened, install malware on the user's computer.

BROWSER ATTACKS:

Browsers are essential for internet access but are often used to deliver malware. Cybercriminals can compromise legitimate websites by injecting malicious code into them. When a user visits an infected website, the malware is downloaded onto their computer.

Some common types of browser attacks include:

- **Drive-by downloads:** This is an attack where the user visits an infected website, and malware is downloaded onto their computer automatically, without their knowledge or consent.

- **Malvertising:** This is where cybercriminals use ads on legitimate websites to deliver malware. They typically use social engineering tactics to trick users into clicking on the ads.

- **Browser plug-in attacks:** This is where cybercriminals create malicious browser plug-ins that users can download and install. These plug-ins can then steal information from the user's computer.

Email and Browser Protection

Email and browser protection are critical aspects of cybersecurity. They play a significant role in safeguarding individuals and organizations against cyber threats like phishing, malware, and other cyber-attacks.

Email Protection:

Email is a popular and convenient mode of communication used by individuals and organizations alike. However, it's also a vulnerable attack vector for cybercriminals. Email protection measures are essential to ensure that your email remains secure.

Here are some email protection measures:

- **Spam filters:** Spam filters are software programs that protect your inbox from unwanted or unsolicited emails, also known as spam. They use multiple techniques to detect and remove spam emails, such as phishing attempts, scams, and promotional messages you didn't ask for. These filters are essential for email protection because they help prevent users from becoming victims of cybercrime, such as phishing attacks and identity theft. Spam filters use a combination of rules and algorithms to identify spam emails. They can analyze email content, sender information, and other factors to determine whether an email is legitimate.

Some common techniques used by spam filters include:

- **Content Filtering:** Email spam filters analyze the content of an email to determine whether it is spam. They can detect certain keywords, phrases, or patterns commonly linked to spam emails.

- **Sender Filtering:** Spam filters can also check the sender's email address to determine whether it is legitimate. They can verify the sender's domain and check for authentication methods like DKIM and SPF (described below) to ensure the email is not spoofed or forged.

- **Reputation Filtering:** Spam filters can also use reputation filtering to determine whether an email is spam. They can check the sender's IP address and domain against known spam lists to determine whether the sender has a history of spamming emails.

Once a spam filter has identified an email as spam, it can take several actions to prevent it from reaching your inbox. These can include:

- **Moving the email to a spam folder:** The spam filter can move the email to a separate folder designated for spam emails. This prevents it from cluttering your inbox and makes it easier to manage unwanted emails.

- **Deleting the email:** In some cases, the spam filter may delete the email outright if it is deemed highly suspicious or dangerous.

- **Quarantining the email:** Some spam filters may quarantine the email, which means it is held in a separate location for some time before it is deleted or released to the user's inbox.

- **Email authentication:** is the process of validating the sender's identity and ensuring that emails are legitimate. It is a crucial part of email protection as it helps prevent email spoofing and other email-related attacks.

Email authentication is done through various protocols, including Domain Keys Identified Mail (DKIM), Sender Policy

Framework (SPF), and Domain-based Message Authentication, Reporting & Conformance (DMARC).

- **Domain Keys Identified Mail (DKIM):**

  DKIM is a method that helps make sure an email is genuine and comes from the correct domain name. It works by adding a unique digital signature to the email, created using a special code (called a private key) linked to the domain name. When someone gets the email, their program looks at this signature and compares it to another code (called a public key) publicly available in the sender's domain record. The email is considered legitimate and safe if the signature is correct.

- **Sender Policy Framework (SPF):**

  SPF is a method that helps make sure an email is sent from a trusted server. It does this using a special record that lists which servers can send emails for a certain domain. When someone gets an email, their program can look at this record to see if it was sent from one of the approved servers. If it was, the email would be seen as legitimate and safe.

- **Domain-based Message Authentication, Reporting & Conformance (DMARC):**

  DMARC is a method that improves email safety by using SPF and DKIM together and adding extra protection against fake emails. With DMARC, the people who own domain names can say how the email programs should treat the emails of those receiving them. DMARC records are added to the domain's information, letting the domain owner decide what to do if an email doesn't pass the SPF or DKIM tests. This helps ensure that only genuine emails are delivered, and fake ones are stopped.

- **Email encryption:**

  This is a critical aspect of cybersecurity. It helps to protect the confidentiality and integrity of sensitive information shared via email. Email encryption works by converting the content of an email message into a code that can only be read by authorized individuals who possess the necessary decryption key.

Browser Protection:

Browser protection is an important aspect of cybersecurity as web browsers are often used as an entry point for cyber-attacks. Malicious websites, pop-ups, and downloads can compromise your system, steal your personal information, and damage your computer.

Here are some browser protection measures you can implement to ensure that you remain safe online:

- **<u>Keep Your Browser Up-to-Date:</u>**

  Browser protection means ensuring that it's up-to-date. Browsers regularly release updates to fix security vulnerabilities and bugs. Keeping your browser up-to-date is essential to ensure it has the latest security features and patches. You can enable automatic updates in your browser settings to ensure you always have the latest version.

- **Use Ad-Blockers:**

  Ad-blockers are browser extensions designed to prevent ads from displaying on your screen. They are effective in blocking malicious ads and pop-ups that may contain malware. Ad-blockers also improve your browsing experience by removing annoying ads and increasing page loading speed.

- **Install Browser Security Extensions:**

  Browser security extensions like HTTPS Everywhere and NoScript can protect your browser from malicious websites and scripts. HTTPS Everywhere encrypts your communications with websites and ensures your data is secure. NoScript blocks scripts from running on your browser, preventing malicious scripts from running on your computer. These extensions can significantly improve your browser's security and protect you from cyber-attacks.

- **Use a VPN:**

  A virtual private network (VPN) is a way to safely connect your computer to the Internet. It encrypts your internet traffic, maintaining your online privacy. Additionally, it can help you avoid internet censorship and access restricted content in your location.

- **Be Cautious of Downloads:**

  Downloading software from untrusted sources can compromise your system. Malicious software can be disguised as legitimate software and infect your computer with malware. Only download software from reputable sources and ensure that you have anti-malware software installed on your system to detect and remove any malware that may have been downloaded.

Malware Defense

The last few breaches I have seen were related to someone opening an email, clicking a link, and infecting the network.

And if someone does hack you to get into your computer, they probably did it with malware. Malware can also steal data, shut down operations and cause damage to your system. There are many types of malware.

TYPES OF MALWARE

Several types of malware are used to carry out malicious activities:

- **Viruses:** Viruses are programs that can replicate themselves and spread from one computer to another. They can corrupt files, steal data, or delete important files on a computer.

- **Trojans:** Trojans are deceptive software programs that pretend to be legitimate, but once installed, they can carry out harmful actions such as stealing passwords, recording keystrokes, or creating backdoors for remote access.

- **Worms:** Worms are self-replicating programs that spread over computer networks, consuming system resources and causing damage to networked systems.

- **Ransomware:** Ransomware has been very successful in the 2010–2020s. It's a dangerous software that encrypts computer files and demands payment for a decryption key. Ransomware can quickly spread across a network and cause serious harm to an organization's data, resulting in data loss, operational disruptions, and financial losses. Implementing effective cybersecurity measures such as software updates, data backups, and cybersecurity awareness training is The best way to protect against ransomware.

- **Adware:** Adware is software that displays unwanted advertisements on a user's computer, often redirecting them to malicious websites.

- **Spyware:** Spyware is software that secretly collects information about a user's activities, such as web browsing habits, and sends it to a remote server without the user's knowledge or consent.

Malware attacks through email and browsers are common methods cybercriminals use to compromise computer systems and steal sensitive information.

HERE ARE SOME OF THE KEY DEFENSES:

- **Endpoint Protection:** Endpoint protection is a critical first defense against malware attacks. Organizations should implement endpoint protection solutions, including anti-virus software, firewalls, and intrusion detection/prevention systems. These solutions can help detect and block malware before it can infect endpoints such as desktops, laptops, servers, and mobile devices. It is important to update these solutions with the latest threat intelligence and regularly test them to ensure they work effectively.

- **Access Control:** Access control is another important defense against malware. By limiting access to sensitive systems and data to only authorized personnel, organizations can reduce the risk of malware infecting these systems or stealing data. Multi-factor authentication (MFA) can strengthen access controls by requiring more than one form of authentication to access sensitive systems and data. This can prevent attackers from gaining access even if they have stolen a user's credentials.

- **Secure Configuration:** Secure configuration ensures that all devices and software are configured securely and updated with the latest patches. This can help mitigate vulnerabilities that could be exploited by malware. Organizations should implement secure configuration standards for all devices and software and regularly audit them to ensure they comply. This can include disabling unnecessary services, configuring firewalls, and setting strong passwords.

- **Incident Response:** Incident response is critical for quickly detecting and responding to malware attacks. Organizations should develop incident response plans that outline the steps to take when malware infects a system or if there is a threat exploiting a weakness. These plans should include procedures for isolating infected systems, restoring data from backups, and conducting a post-incident review to identify and remediate vulnerabilities that allowed the malware to enter in the first place.

- **Data Protection:** Data protection measures such as encryption, access controls, and backups can help prevent data loss or theft in case of a malware attack. Encryption can protect data at rest and in transit, while access controls can prevent unauthorized access to sensitive data. Regularly backing up data can ensure that data can be restored in case of data loss or corruption caused by malware.

- **Security Awareness Training:** Security awareness training is a key line of defense against malware. Employees can be taught to recognize and avoid malware dangers like phishing emails and dubious websites. This can lessen the possibility of human error-related malware infiltration.

Security Framework Reference to Email, Browsers & Malware

NIST 800-53 security controls address malware in SI-3, malicious protection. Multiple security controls can help security browsers, but the main ones on NIST are SI-8, spam protection, and SI-2, flaw remediation.

The CIS Critical controls cover email, browsers, and malware with CIS Control 9, Email & Browser Protection, and CIS Control 10, Malware Defense.

Email, Browser & Malware Control Training & Resources

Here are some training resources for email, browser, and malware security:

- Coursera - Email and Messaging Security: A course provided by the University of Colorado that covers email security, messaging protocols, encryption, and best practices for secure communication. (https://www.coursera.org/learn/email-messaging-security)

- Pluralsight - Email Security Fundamentals: This course offers insights into email security concepts, including email security protocols, spam filtering, and phishing protection techniques. (https://www.pluralsight.com/courses/email-security-fundamentals)

- Cybrary - Email Security Course: Offers a free online course that covers email security, including topics such as encryption, authentication, and protection against phishing attacks. (https://www.cybrary.it/course/email-security/)

- Coursera - Web Security Fundamentals: The University of Michigan provides a course covering browser security, web vulnerabilities, and best practices for securing web applications. Web Security Fundamentals

- Pluralsight - Browser Security Course: This course offers insights into browser security concepts, including same-origin policy, cross-site scripting (XSS) protection, and secure browsing techniques. Browser Security Course

- Cybrary - Web Application Security Course: Offers a free online course that covers web application security, including topics such as browser security, web vulnerabilities, and secure coding practices. Cybrary Web Application Security Course

- Coursera - Malware Analysis and Defense: The University of London provides a course covering malware types, analysis techniques, and defense strategies to protect systems from malicious software. (https://www.coursera.org/learn/malware-analysis-defense)

- Pluralsight - Defending Against Malware: This course offers insights into malware defense concepts, including malware detection, analysis, and remediation techniques. (https://www.pluralsight.com/courses/defending-against-malware)

- Cybrary - Malware Analysis Course: Offers a free online course that covers malware analysis and defense, including topics such as reverse engineering, dynamic analysis, and static analysis. (https://www.cybrary.it/course/malware-analysis/)

CHAPTER 6

Data Protection & Recovery

I had RAID!

RAID isn't backup

> **"The best way to get management excited about a disaster plan is to burn down the building across the street."**
>
> ~Dan Erwin,
> Security Officer, Dow Chemical Co.

The cool thing about Batman is that he is always ready. That's his power; he's always 10 steps ahead of everyone. He even has a contingency plan to remove the entire Justice League if necessary. Organizations need to be the same way with data.

They must think about what could happen to their data and then take steps to protect and recover.

Data Protection

Data protection is all about keeping sensitive information safe from prying eyes. Previously, companies could keep their data secure within their physical borders. But now, with so much information stored in the cloud and on portable devices, it takes more work to control where that data goes and who has access to it.

Data protection is critical to keep sensitive information, such as financial records, intellectual property, and personal data, private to prevent unauthorized access by individuals or organizations. Additionally, there are often laws and regulations governing the protection of personal data that companies must adhere to.

Attackers look for ways to get their hands on sensitive data, and once they've breached a company's security measures, one of their priorities is to find and steal that data. This can happen through network attacks or physical theft of devices like laptops and smartphones.

To combat these threats, companies must have a plan to manage their data throughout its lifecycle. This includes everything from classifying data based on sensitivity to setting guidelines for protecting, handling, and eventually disposing of it. It's also important to have a breach response plan in place if sensitive data is compromised.

One key aspect of data protection is encryption. Encryption can help prevent data from being compromised during transmission or at rest. Companies may also use labels like "Sensitive," "Confidential," and "Public" to classify their data based on its level of sensitivity.

Companies should also separate their network so that assets with the same sensitivity level are on the same network and separated from those with different sensitivity levels. In addition, firewalls and access controls should be implemented to ensure that only those who need access to sensitive data are allowed access.

Data protection is safeguarding sensitive information from unauthorized access, use, disclosure, modification, or destruction; the organization is protecting the C.I.A of the information. Data protection is essential for any organization that collects, processes, stores, or transmits data that could cause harm or loss to individuals or businesses if compromised. Data protection also helps organizations comply with legal and regulatory requirements that govern the privacy and security of personal data.

Here is an example of data protection. ABC Inc. is a company that provides online services to customers and stores their personal and financial data in a cloud-based database. The company wants to protect its data from cyber attackers' unauthorized access, modification, or deletion. ABC Inc. implements the CIS 3 data protection Safeguards as part of the CIS Controls v8 framework. They can use this control standard to guide their local policies and procedure.

The company has to set up data protection by doing the following:

- Using a data discovery tool to scan its cloud database and identify the types and locations of sensitive data, such as names, addresses, credit card numbers, etc.

- Deleting or archiving any sensitive data that is no longer needed or used by the company or its customers

- Implementing role-based access control (RBAC) policies to limit who can access sensitive data based on their job functions and responsibilities

- Encrypting the sensitive data both at rest (in the database) and in transit (when transferred over the network) using strong encryption algorithms and keys

- Performing regular backups of the sensitive data to a secure location and testing the restoration process periodically

- Deploying a data loss prevention (DLP) solution to monitor the access and usage of sensitive data and alerting the security team of any suspicious or anomalous activities

By protecting data, ABC Inc. can reduce the risk of data breaches, comply with regulatory requirements, and maintain customer trust and satisfaction.

Data Recovery

In all my years of doing IT, I've learned that it's not "IF" your system will go down; it's "WHEN." Usually, it's not even a cyber-attack; it's a hardware failure or one guy that knew everything leaves, and there is no documentation or training for people taking their place. The information will not be accessible for all the reasons.

Losing data can be very annoying and stressful. Imagine you were working on a crucial report or a homework assignment, and your computer suddenly stopped working or restarted. Or you tried to save a file, but it got corrupted or overwritten.

Cybersecurity experts use the term data recovery to restore data that has been lost, corrupted, or deleted from a storage device. A storage device stores data, such as a hard drive, a solid-state drive (SSD), a flash drive, or a memory card. Data loss can happen for various reasons, such as human error, software error, hardware error, malicious attack, or natural calamity.

Data recovery requires special software or hardware tools to access the storage device and recover the data. The complexity and time of data recovery vary depending on how much damage there is to the device and how powerful the tools are.

Data recovery and continuity of operations go hand in hand to help the organization by ensuring that even when things are not going well, the mission or business can keep going. So, your organization can survive and bounce back even with a cyber-attack. Continuity keeps your core functions, operations, and services running during a cyber-attack. At the same time, recovery is the ability to resume normal operations after the attack. To achieve continuity and recovery in cybersecurity, you need to have a plan that covers how to detect and respond to cyber threats, how to protect your essential functions and services during an attack, and how to restore your normal operations after the attack is resolved. A continuity and recovery plan in cybersecurity will help you prepare for and deal with cyber-attacks effectively.

Here are reasons why these aspects are crucial:

- Minimizing Downtime: One of the main reasons why continuity and recovery planning are so important is that they help organizations minimize downtime. Downtime can be costly, resulting in lost revenue, decreased productivity, and damage to an organization's reputation. Plans to quickly recover from a cyber-attack help an organization minimize downtime's impact and return to normal operations.

- Maintaining Business Operations: A continuity and recovery plan is crucial for organizations to sustain their critical functions and operations during a cyber-attack. This involves maintaining essential systems, data, and services for daily operations. With established plans in place, organizations can reduce the impact of an attack by ensuring the continuity of these functions.

- Regulatory Compliance: Many industries are subject to important regulatory requirements that mandate continuity and recovery planning. For example, the healthcare industry must have plans to ensure that patient data remains secure during an attack. Failure to comply with these requirements can result in significant fines and other penalties.

Below are some useful suggestions for establishing an effective Data Recovery:

Data Backups. Define a data recovery process that covers which assets need to be backed up, how often, where to store the backups, and how to restore them securely. Update this process at least once a year or when significant changes occur. Automating the backup is the best solution for making sure they get done.

Test your Backups. Test the backup recovery process regularly, at least once every three months, for a sample of the assets in scope for data recovery. This can help ensure the backup data is valid and can be restored quickly and accurately.

Protect Backups. A few things can be done to protect backups, including encrypting and putting them on an isolated network.

Security Framework Reference to Data Protection & Recovery

NIST 800-53 covers data recovery with CP-9, Information System Backup. Data protection is covered in multiple NIST 800-53 SC and SI controls dealing with encryption and handling sensitive data. The CIS Critical controls have CIS Control 11, which covers data recovery for an organization, and CIS Control 3, data protection.

Data Protection, Recovery Control Training & Resources

Here is some recommended data protection and recovery training resources:

- Coursera - Data Protection and Privacy Regulations: The University of Groningen provides a course covering data protection principles, privacy regulations, and best practices for securing personal data. (https://www.coursera.org/learn/data-protection-privacy-regulations)

- Udemy - General Data Protection Regulation (GDPR) Training: This course offers insights into GDPR compliance, protection principles, and best data security practices. (https://www.udemy.com/course/gdpr-training/)

- Pluralsight - Protecting Data: This course provides information on various data protection techniques, including encryption, hashing, and access control mechanisms. (https://www.pluralsight.com/courses/protecting-data)

- Cybrary - Data Privacy Course: Offers a free online course that covers data privacy and protection, including topics such as privacy regulations, data protection principles, and secure data handling. (https://www.cybrary.it/course/data-privacy/)

- LinkedIn Learning - Data Privacy Foundations: This course explores the fundamentals of data privacy, including data protection regulations, privacy frameworks, and best practices for securing personal data. (https://www.linkedin.com/learning/data-privacy-foundations)

- Coursera - Data Backup and Recovery: The University of Colorado provides a course covering data backup and recovery concepts, strategies, and best practices for ensuring data availability and resilience. https://www.coursera.org/learn/data-backup-recovery)

- Udemy - Data Backup and Recovery Course: This course offers insights into various data backup and recovery techniques, including local and cloud-based backups, disaster recovery planning, and best practices. (https://www.udemy.com/course/data-backup-and-recovery-course/)

- Pluralsight - Backup and Recovery Fundamentals: This course provides information on various data backup and recovery techniques, including backup types, strategies, and disaster recovery planning. (https://www.pluralsight.com/courses/backup-recovery-fundamentals)

- LinkedIn Learning - Backup and Recovery: This course explores the fundamentals of data backup and recovery, including backup types, storage options, and disaster recovery planning. (https://www.linkedin.com/learning/backup-and-recovery)

- Veeam - Backup and Recovery Training: Veeam offers training courses and resources on data backup and recovery, focusing on their backup and disaster recovery solutions for virtualized environments. (https://www.veeam.com/education-services.html)

CHAPTER 7

NETWORK SECURITY

> **The ARPAnet was the first transcontinental, high-speed computer network.**
>
> ~Eric S. Raymond

According to Pew Research Center, 97% of people in the US own a cell phone (as of 2021). Globally, it's about 85%, which means most people are on a network. It's a huge part of our lives that we don't think about, like electricity. The credit system relies on a network when you pay with credit to the store. All television shows you watch are broadcast using a network. And even if you don't have a phone or watch TV and pay for everything with cash, someone you exchange money with at some point has to go to a bank, which uses a network. My point is humanity relies on computer networks a lot.

A computer network is a collection of computers, devices, and servers connected through various communication channels. This allows them to share data, resources, and information. Networks can be wired or wireless and are often used in homes, offices, and across the internet to facilitate communication and collaboration.

Unfortunately, many of these devices can be vulnerable to attackers trying to gain unauthorized access. To protect these devices, network security involves using various software and hardware tools that can be installed on a network or used as a service. As networks become more complex and businesses rely more on them, security becomes even more crucial. This means that security methods must keep up with new attack methods created by malicious actors seeking to exploit these increasingly complex networks.

Network security is safeguarding a computer network and the data stored on it. The importance of network security cannot be overstated because it helps to keep sensitive data safe from hackers and other cybercriminals. It also ensures that the network remains reliable and trustworthy for its intended users.

To achieve effective network security, it is crucial to implement a combination of security measures to protect against various cyber threats. This includes malware and distributed denial of service attacks, common types of cyber-attacks that can cause serious harm to a network and the data it holds. By implementing multiple layers of security, organizations and users can be better protected against these threats and ensure the safety and reliability of their networks.

Key Components of Network Security

- **Access control**: This involves limiting access to resources on a network based on a user's identity and authorization level. Access control can be achieved through authentication mechanisms, such as passwords, biometric identification, or digital certificates.

- **Firewalls:** A firewall is a network security device that monitors and filters incoming and outgoing traffic based on predefined rules. It is a barrier between the internal network and the Internet or other external networks.

- **Intrusion prevention/detection systems:** These security systems detect and prevent unauthorized access to a network. They can be configured to identify known attack signatures, strange behavior, or other suspicious activity.

- **Virtual private networks (VPNs):** A secure, encrypted connection allows users to access a private network over a public network, such as the Internet. It provides a secure network connection to remote users or offices.

- **Encryption** is the process of encoding data so that only authorized parties can access it. Encryption can be used to protect data transmitted over a network, as well as data stored on devices.

- **Security policies:** Network security policies outline the rules and guidelines that govern how a network should be accessed and used. They can include password policies, acceptable use policies, and incident response procedures.

Network Management

Organizations can improve their overall network security posture by developing an inventory of network devices, creating network diagrams, implementing access controls, monitoring network traffic, configuring network devices securely, and implementing network segmentation.

The organization should follow a network security policy to ensure a set approach to securing the network infrastructure. This helps guarantee the consistent implementation of security controls across the organization, reducing the risk of security breaches and potential data breaches.

Network Infrastructure Procedures and Tools:

- **Establish Network Security Policies**

  Network security policies set the standard for the entire network infrastructure. It involves defining the organization's network security objectives, responsibilities, and procedures. This includes developing policies for access control, network segmentation, and wireless network security. The policies should be clear, concise, and aligned with the organization's security strategy. The policies should also be reviewed and updated regularly to remain relevant and effective.

- **Inventory Network Devices**

  Inventorying network devices involves creating a list of all network devices, including routers, switches, servers, and other devices. This inventory should include the device name, model, firmware version, IP address, and location. This inventory is essential for effective network monitoring and management. The inventory should be updated regularly to reflect any changes to the network infrastructure.

- **Implement Wireless Network Security**

  Proper security management of the network should also consider the wireless network when present. Wireless access point devices must be purchased from approved vendors supporting hardware and firmware. To ensure the confidentiality and integrity of all data on the wireless network, it is crucial to implement network segregation and robust encryption methods.

- **Implement Network Segmentation**

  Dividing the network into smaller subnetworks or segments limits the scope of potential attacks and prevents lateral movement by attackers. This helps to contain any damage that may occur in a security breach.

- **Regularly Update and Patch Network Devices**

  Regularly updating and patching network devices is critical for maintaining a secure network infrastructure. This process involves applying security patches and firmware updates, as well as updating configuration files and implementing new security controls. Organizations can protect against known vulnerabilities by keeping network devices up-to-date and enhancing security.

- **Develop Incident Response Procedures**

  Developing incident response procedures is essential for effective network security. This includes establishing procedures for detecting, responding to, and recovering from security incidents and establishing roles and responsibilities for incident response. In addition, incident response procedures help ensure that the organization is prepared to respond to security incidents promptly and effectively.

- **Perform Security Audits and Penetration Testing**

  Performing security audits and penetration testing is critical to identifying vulnerabilities and weaknesses in the network infrastructure. This includes conducting vulnerability assessments, penetration testing, and security audits regularly. Security audits and penetration testing help to identify vulnerabilities and weaknesses in the network infrastructure so that they can be addressed before attackers can exploit them.

Network Monitoring

Network monitoring enables an organization to identify any suspicious or anomalous activity in their network, such as unauthorized access attempts or data exfiltration attempts. By monitoring the network in real-time, an organization can detect potential threats early and take necessary actions to mitigate them.

In addition to detecting potential threats, network monitoring helps an organization understand its traffic patterns, identify congestion or inefficiencies, and optimize network performance. This helps to ensure that the network infrastructure is functioning effectively and efficiently.

Network Monitoring Tools

Network monitoring has powerful tools that have whole careers built around them.

- **Network Security Monitoring (NSM) Tools**

  NSM tools enable the monitoring and analysis of network traffic to detect potential threats and security incidents. These tools can capture network traffic, perform protocol analysis, and identify suspicious activity. Examples of NSM tools include Snort, Suricata, and Zeek.

- **Intrusion Detection and Prevention Systems (IDPS)**

  IDPS tools can detect and prevent potential security incidents, such as intrusion attempts, malware infections, and suspicious traffic patterns. They can also alert security personnel to respond quickly to potential threats. Examples of IDPS tools include Cisco Firepower, McAfee Network Security Platform, and Check Point IPS.

- **Security Information and Event Management (SIEM) Systems**

  SIEM systems collect and analyze security data from various sources, such as network devices, servers, and applications. This helps to identify potential threats and respond to them promptly. SIEM systems can also provide security analytics and reporting capabilities. Examples of SIEM systems include Splunk, IBM QRadar, and LogRhythm.

- **ENDPOINT DETECTION AND RESPONSE (EDR) TOOLS**

    EDR tools can monitor and analyze endpoint activities to detect potential security incidents, such as malware infections and suspicious behavior. They can also alert security personnel to respond to potential threats quickly. Examples of EDR tools include Carbon Black, CrowdStrike, and Symantec Endpoint Protection.

Security Framework References for Network Security

Some best security practices are not addressed in some frameworks. For example, even with over one thousand controls, the NIST 800-53 revision 5 does not cover how to protect credit card readers or cloud systems. But ALL frameworks in every industry address network security.

CIS Control 12 is a set of guidelines and recommendations to help organizations secure their network infrastructure. This control ensures organizations have the necessary procedures and tools to monitor, manage, and secure their network infrastructure effectively. CIS 13 (Network Monitoring and Defense) is a security control in the CIS Controls V8 framework. It involves monitoring and defending the network against potential cyber threats, such as unauthorized access, malware infections, and suspicious activity. For federal systems, the NIST 800 has control SC System And Communications Protection. System and Communications Protection refers to guidelines and measures that help safeguard computer systems and their communication channels. It involves implementing security controls to protect sensitive data, prevent unauthorized access, and maintain system integrity. Simply put, it's about keeping computer systems and the information they share safe from threats and ensuring their communication remains secure and confidential.

Network Training References

This is one concept that requires that you know more of a deeper technical understanding to know how to protect computer networks. The deeper you go, the more you can help protect it. Although many layers go into many different paths (from developing wide area networks for fortune 500 companies to doing packet analysis for governments), I would suggest you at least have a solid grasp of the basics. Here is a list of resources to get you started:

1. Cisco Networking Academy (https://www.netacad.com): Offers courses on networking fundamentals and certification preparation.

2. Coursera (https://www.coursera.org): Provides various online courses on computer networks and related topics taught by experts from top universities.

3. edX (https://www.edx.org): Offers a range of networking courses from universities and institutions worldwide.

4. CompTIA Network+ Certification (https://www.comptia.org/certifications/network): A well-recognized certification that covers network fundamentals and best practices.

5. YouTube Channels (e.g., NetworkChuck, Eli the Computer Guy, Professor Messer): Offer free video tutorials on networking topics.

6. "Computer Networks" by Andrew S. Tanenbaum: A popular textbook that covers the basics of computer networks and their protocols.

7. Wireshark (https://www.wireshark.org): A network protocol analyzer that allows you to study and understand network traffic in real time.

8. Networking for Dummies by Doug Lowe: A beginner-friendly book that introduces networking concepts in a simplified manner.

9. Stack Exchange Network Engineering (https://networkengineering.stackexchange.com): A Q&A platform for network professionals to ask and answer questions about networking.

10. Internet Engineering Task Force (IETF) (https://www.ietf.org): The organization responsible for developing and promoting internet standards, including various networking protocols. You can access their RFCs (Request for Comments) to learn more about the underlying technologies that power the internet.

CHAPTER 8

SECURITY AWARENESS

"The methods that will most effectively minimize the ability of intruders to compromise information security are comprehensive user training and education. Enacting policies and procedures simply won't suffice. Even with oversight the policies and procedures may not be effective: my access to Motorola, Nokia, ATT, Sun depended upon the willingness of people to bypass policies and procedures that were in place for years before I compromised them successfully."

~Kevin Mitnick

Many data breaches come from social engineering. Criminal hackers trick users into giving up their credentials. Ignorant users are usually the weakest link on a network. If users can be tricked into giving access, it doesn't matter how much network security or firewalls you have.

Cybersecurity training in an organization refers to educating staff on the best practices and techniques for preventing, detecting, and responding to cyber threats. This includes providing training on various aspects of cybersecurity, such as network security, data protection, password management, phishing awareness, and incident response.

Cybersecurity training aims to equip all staff members with a fundamental knowledge of the organization's cyber threats and how to lessen those risks. It's worth noting that cybersecurity training shouldn't only be restricted to the IT department. Every staff member is responsible for safeguarding the organization's systems and data security.

The training should be comprehensive and cover all aspects of the organization, including technical and non-technical staff. This means that the training should be tailored to the needs of different departments and staff members, depending on their roles and responsibilities.

It's important to have ongoing cybersecurity training that is frequently reviewed and updated to stay current with the latest risks and best practices. One-time training isn't sufficient as it's hard for staff to remember everything they learned. To ensure that personnel are informed about the latest threats and how to reduce them, refresher courses and updated training materials should be provided regularly.

The following is an overview of the training process in an organization in cyber security:

- **Identify the training needs:** Before training can occur, the organization must identify the specific cybersecurity training needs. This can be done through a risk assessment, vulnerability scan, or penetration testing. The organization should determine which areas of cybersecurity are the most important to address and what type of training is required.

- **Develop a training plan:** Once the training needs have been identified, the organization should develop a training plan that outlines the topics, methods, and goals of the training. The plan should also include a timeline and budget for the training.

- **Select training methods:** Several training methods can be used to train staff in cybersecurity. These methods include online courses, classroom training, workshops, seminars, and simulations. The organization should choose the most appropriate method for its staff and the training goals.

- **Implement the training:** Once the training plan has been developed and the training methods have been selected, the organization can begin implementing the training. The training should be mandatory for all staff with access to sensitive information or critical systems.

- **Evaluate the training:** The organization should evaluate its effectiveness after completing it. This can be done through surveys or assessments that measure the staff's knowledge before and after the training. The evaluation will help the organization determine if the training was effective and if any changes need to be made for future training.

- **Update the training:** Cybersecurity threats are constantly evolving, so it is essential that the training is updated regularly. The organization should review the training plan and make necessary changes to ensure the staff is trained on the latest threats and best practices.

Implementing a Security Awareness Program

Security awareness training is often a part of security compliance. The training needs to be a part of a security awareness program. It should be documented in a policy and completed regularly in a process that affects everyone in the organization.

The organization's security awareness program should ensure that every employee is aware of the correct behavior that will contribute to the upkeep of the organization's security and that they exhibit it. Annual training may be sufficient in some circumstances, but more frequent refreshers may be required if employees are unfamiliar with security measures. Some of the things that should go into the training program include:

- **Train employees on how to spot social engineering attacks**

  The next best practice is educating your workforce about social engineering attacks and how to spot them. Cover all possible attack types, such as phishing, impersonation, and phone scams.

- **Train Workforce Members on Authentication Best Practices**

  To keep your system and data safe, it's crucial to have secure authentication measures in place. All members of your workforce need to understand the significance of secure authentication and the potential risks of not following corporate processes. Some commonly used types of authentication include:

  - Password-based authentication
  - Multifactor authentication
  - Certificate-based authentication

- **Train the workforce on security best practices for data handling**

  Employees need training on the proper handling of sensitive data, including recognizing, storing, archiving, transferring, and destroying sensitive data. Basic instruction may include teaching employees to lock their displays when leaving their computers and erase private information from virtual whiteboards during meetings.

- **Train the Workforce about Unintentional Data Exposure**

  Mobile device loss, sending the wrong email to the wrong person, and keeping data in locations where authorized people can access it are all examples of unintended data exposure. Ensure your staff members know their publishing options and how crucial it is to exercise care when utilizing email and mobile devices.

- **Train the Workforce on how to Recognize and Handle Security Incidents**

  Designate a single point of contact for incident reporting to streamline the process. Educate employees on how to identify missing security updates and report them. Teach employees to test systems, identify outdated software patches, and consult with IT staff before accepting or rejecting updates. Educate employees on the risks of connecting to unreliable networks and ensure remote workers receive extra training on securing their home networks.

The overall goal of the security awareness program is to increase employee awareness, improve security posture, support compliance, and integrate cybersecurity into the organization's culture.

Security Framework Reference to Security Awareness & Training

NIST 800-53, AT, security awareness training, addresses how federal organizations should continuously train users with access to the network.

For CIS Critical Controls version 8, it's CIS 14, also known as Security Awareness and Skills Training. This control is a security standard developed by the Center for Internet Security (CIS) to promote awareness and skills training for individuals within organizations. The standard provides guidelines for establishing and maintaining an effective security awareness and training program that mitigate the risks associated with threats.

Security Awareness Training Resources

Here are some resources to help your organization create a security awareness training program.

- HHS Security Awareness & Training: The U.S. Department of Health and Human Services provides security awareness training for employees, contractors, and other stakeholders. [HHS Security Awareness & Training] (https://www.hhs.gov/about/agencies/asa/ocio/cyberse curity/security-awareness-training/index.html)

- SANS Securing the Human - Security Awareness Training: SANS offers a comprehensive training program to educate users about cybersecurity threats and best practices. [SANS Security Awareness Training] (https://www.sans.org/security-awareness-training)

- KnowBe4 - Security Awareness Training: KnowBe4 provides a platform for training and phishing simulations to help organizations assess and improve their employees' security awareness. [KnowBe4 Security Awareness Training] (https://www.knowbe4.com/security-awareness-training)

- Infosec - Security Awareness and Training: Infosec offers a comprehensive security awareness training platform called Infosec IQ that includes training modules, assessments, and phishing simulations. [Infosec Security Awareness and Training] (https://www.infosecinstitute.com/iq)

- Cybrary - End User Security Awareness Training: Cybrary provides a free security awareness training course designed for end users, covering topics such as password security, email security, and social engineering. [Cybrary End User Security Awareness] (https://www.cybrary.it/course/end-user-security-awareness/)

- Proofpoint - Security Awareness Training: Proofpoint offers a training program that includes interactive modules, phishing simulations, and reporting tools to help organizations improve their employees' security awareness. [Proofpoint Security Awareness Training] (https://www.proofpoint.com/us/products/security-awareness-training)

- ESET - Cybersecurity Awareness Training: ESET offers a free training course designed for organizations to educate their employees on key cybersecurity topics, such as phishing, social engineering, and password security. [ESET Cybersecurity Awareness Training] (https://www.eset.com/us/cybertraining/)

- Mimecast - Security Awareness Training: Mimecast provides a security awareness training platform that includes engaging video content, assessments, and phishing simulations to help organizations reduce employee-related security risks. [Mimecast Security Awareness Training] (https://www.mimecast.com/products/security-awareness-training/)

- Terranova Security - Security Awareness Training: Terranova Security offers a comprehensive training program that includes interactive modules, phishing simulations, and assessments to help organizations improve their security posture. [Terranova Security Awareness Training] (https://terranovasecurity.com/security-awareness-training/)

- Webroot - Security Awareness Training: Webroot provides a security awareness training platform that includes engaging content, phishing simulations, and progress tracking to help organizations reduce security risks associated with employee behavior. [Webroot Security Awareness Training] (https://www.webroot.com/us/en/business/security-awareness)

CHAPTER 9

Cloud Security

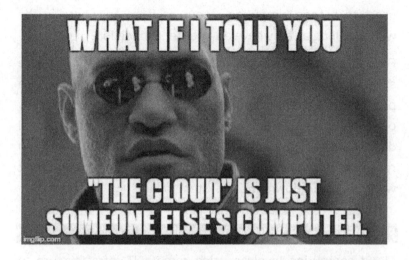

"Cloud computing is a no-brainer for any start-up because it allows you to test your business plan very quickly for little money. Every start-up, or even a division within a company that has an idea for something new, should be figuring out how to use cloud computing in its plan."

~Brad Jefferson, CEO Animoto

Cloud technology is an essential component of modern computing infrastructure. Cloud computing enables businesses and individuals to access computing resources such as processing power, storage, and applications through a network of remote servers that service providers manage.

Cloud service providers offer a scalable solution for businesses and individuals, allowing them to quickly and easily increase or decrease their computing resources as needed. This means that users only pay for what they use. Cloud technology enables users to access computing resources from anywhere in the world, as long as they have an internet connection.

For some organizations, buying cloud services is more affordable than hosting all services on their site. The service providers are also very good at reliability. The providers typically offer high reliability and uptime, with redundant systems and data centers in multiple locations. This means that users can rely on the service to be available when they need it without worrying about downtime or system failures.

Popular Cloud Solutions

Cloud computing involves using remote IT infrastructure to deliver various services, and there are four main types of cloud solutions. These four pillars of cloud services include:

IAAS

Infrastructure as a Service (IaaS) is a versatile cloud service where clients are given a complete computing infrastructure managed online by the provider. It supports various tools for business operations and avoids the hassle of in-house IT infrastructure. IaaS offers scalable computing resources, including virtual machines, storage, and networking services, for a flexible, cost-effective solution to improve organizational operations.

PAAS

PaaS, short for Platform as a Service, is a specialized cloud service that provides developers with the tools to develop and manage software products. A PaaS includes everything a developer needs to create an app, including development tools, management systems, and operating systems. This cloud service is particularly beneficial for companies that need to build custom applications as it is more cost effective than purchasing all the necessary tools individually. Additionally, PaaS facilitates collaboration among remote teams, which can accelerate the production process. One of the main advantages of PaaS is that it allows developers to build, test, and deploy applications without worrying about managing the underlying infrastructure.

SAAS

Software as a Service is a cloud computing solution that provides fully functional software to clients. By subscribing to SaaS, organizations can access a specific software solution that caters to their needs. What's great about SaaS is that it doesn't require downloading or installing large data files. Most SaaS apps are accessible directly from a web browser. Managed by the CSP, SaaS solutions are monitored and maintained by a service provider, freeing up staff to focus on other tasks. SaaS gives users access to software applications hosted and managed by the service provider.

FAAS

Function as a Service (FaaS) is a cloud service that's not as commonly used as other solutions. FaaS is a cloud service family that enables clients to execute code quickly without allocating resources beforehand. It's aptly named FaaS, as it's designed to help with the execution of a specific function when required.

Cloud technology also includes various tools and technologies that facilitate cloud computing, such as containerization, serverless, and edge computing. With containerization, developers can package their applications and dependencies into portable containers, which can be run on any platform supporting containerization. Serverless computing allows developers to run code without managing servers, as the cloud provider manages the infrastructure. And Edge computing involves processing data closer to the source, reducing the latency of transmitting data to remote servers.

Major cloud service providers include Microsoft Azure, Amazon Web Services (AWS), Microsoft Azure, Google Cloud Platform, IBM Cloud, and Alibaba Cloud.

- **Amazon Web Services (AWS):** AWS is the largest cloud service provider, offering a wide range of services and solutions, including IaaS, PaaS, and SaaS. AWS provides a broad range of computing, storage, and database services and analytics, machine learning, and Internet of Things (IoT) services. AWS also offers many tools and services for developers, such as AWS Lambda, AWS Elastic Beanstalk, and AWS Code Pipeline.

- **Microsoft Azure:** Azure is Microsoft's cloud computing platform that offers services, including IaaS, PaaS, and

SaaS. Azure provides computing, storage, and database services and services for machine learning, analytics, and IoT. Azure also offers a variety of tools and services for developers, such as Azure Functions, Azure App Service, and Azure DevOps.

- **Google Cloud Platform (GCP):** Google's cloud computing platform includes a wide range of services, including IaaS, PaaS, and SaaS. GCP provides computing, storage, and database services and services for machine learning, analytics, and IoT. GCP also offers a variety of tools and services for developers, such as Google Cloud Functions, Google App Engine, and Google Cloud Build.

- **IBM Cloud:** IBM Cloud includes IaaS, PaaS, and SaaS. IBM Cloud provides computing, storage, and database services and services for machine learning, analytics, and IoT. IBM Cloud also offers a variety of tools and services for developers, such as IBM Cloud Functions, IBM Cloud Foundry, and IBM DevOps.

- **Alibaba Cloud:** China's top cloud platform is Alibaba Cloud which includes IaaS, PaaS, and SaaS. Alibaba Cloud provides computing, storage, and database services and services for machine learning, analytics, and IoT. Alibaba Cloud also offers a variety of tools and services for developers, such as Function Compute, Container Service, and DevOps.

Securing cloud-based systems involves implementing the same best security practices as other systems. These include having an incident response plan, security policies, monitoring, vulnerability management, secure configurations, and other fundamental security features. The key distinction lies in tailoring the implementation to suit the cloud environment.

For example, you can create and manage virtual servers on an AWS cloud-based system using the Amazon Elastic Compute Cloud (EC2) service. To secure these servers, you should follow best practices such as disabling unnecessary services, restricting open ports, and limiting server access using security groups. Security groups act as virtual firewalls, controlling inbound and outbound traffic to your EC2 instances. You can also use AWS Identity and Access Management (IAM) to create user accounts with role-based permissions, ensuring users have the least privilege necessary to perform their tasks.

Another example of applying security on a cloud system would be regularly scanning your cloud resources for vulnerabilities is essential. You can use AWS-native tools like AWS Inspector to perform automated security assessments of your EC2 instances. AWS Inspector checks your instances against predefined security rules and generates a detailed report of security findings. You can apply necessary patches or updates to address the identified vulnerabilities based on the findings. Additionally, you should monitor AWS Security Bulletins and announcements for any new threats or vulnerabilities related to AWS services and apply recommended mitigations.

Security Framework Reference to Cloud

Several security frameworks and standards address cloud security to help organizations protect their data, applications, and infrastructure in cloud environments. Some of the most widely recognized frameworks include:

- Cloud Security Alliance (CSA) Cloud Controls Matrix (CCM): CSA CCM is a comprehensive framework that provides a detailed set of security controls designed for cloud computing. It covers various aspects of cloud security, such as data protection, identity and access management, and incident response.

- CSA STAR (Security, Trust, Assurance, and Risk) Program: The CSA STAR Program is a certification and attestation program that offers organizations a way to assess and validate the security posture of their cloud service providers (CSPs). It incorporates the CSA CCM and other cloud security best practices.

- NIST SP 500-291: This NIST publication, also known as the NIST Cloud Computing Standards Roadmap, provides guidance on the security standards and frameworks that apply to cloud computing environments. It helps organizations identify and adopt relevant security controls for their cloud deployments.

- ISO/IEC 27018: This standard offers a code of practice for protecting personally identifiable information (PII) in public cloud environments. It outlines best practices for CSPs to ensure data privacy and compliance with data protection regulations.

These security frameworks guide organizations to implement effective cloud security controls and measures, ensuring their cloud resources' confidentiality, integrity, and availability.

Cloud Training & Resources

Here are some sites to learn about cloud computing:

- AWS Certified Cloud Practitioner: Amazon Web Services provides a certification for cloud practitioners, which includes training materials, whitepapers, and sample exam questions. (https://aws.amazon.com/certification/certified-cloud-practitioner/)

- Coursera - Cloud Computing Specialization: This specialization, offered by the University of Illinois, covers essential cloud computing concepts, including distributed systems, big data, and cloud application development. (https://www.coursera.org/specializations/cloud-computing)

- Microsoft Learn - Azure Fundamentals: Microsoft provides a learning path that covers Azure cloud fundamentals, including core services, management tools, and basic architecture. (https://docs.microsoft.com/en-us/learn/paths/azure-fundamentals/)

- Google Cloud Training - Fundamentals: Google offers training resources that cover the fundamentals of Google Cloud Platform services, including computing, storage, and networking. (https://cloud.google.com/training/fundamentals)

- Udemy - Cloud Computing Courses: Udemy offers various courses on cloud computing, including AWS, Azure, and Google Cloud, covering both foundational concepts and more advanced topics. (https://www.udemy.com/topic/cloud-computing/)

- edX - Cloud Computing Courses: edX provides a variety of cloud computing courses, including those from top institutions like Harvard, MIT, and Berkeley, covering topics such as cloud architecture, security, and big data. (https://www.edx.org/learn/cloud-computing)

- Pluralsight - Cloud Computing Courses: Pluralsight offers a library of cloud computing courses covering major cloud platforms like AWS, Azure, and Google Cloud, as well as fundamental concepts and best practices. (https://www.pluralsight.com/browse/cloud-computing)

- A Cloud Guru: A Cloud Guru is a platform that offers cloud computing training courses for various cloud platforms, including AWS, Azure, and Google Cloud, as well as certification exam preparation. (https://acloudguru.com/)

- Cloud Academy: Cloud Academy provides a comprehensive learning platform for cloud computing, including courses, hands-on labs, and certification exam preparation for AWS, Azure, and Google Cloud. (https://cloudacademy.com/)

- Linux Academy: Linux Academy offers cloud computing courses and certification exam preparation for major cloud platforms, including AWS, Azure, and Google Cloud, along with Linux and DevOps training. (https://linuxacademy.com/)

CHAPTER 10

APPLICATION SECURITY (AppSec)

> **"You are an essential ingredient in our ongoing effort to reduce Security Risk."**
>
> ~Kirsten Manthorne

Today you have probably used 20 different apps and didn't even realize it. If you listen to an audiobook, read an ebook, or open a PDF, you use a few applications. If you interact with your bank, you have had to use an application; I am not just talking about a mobile app. The ATM has an application that runs on an operating system, and the bank teller uses an application to deposit and withdraw cash.

Maybe you don't use a smartphone. Even so, you have used an app because many of the things we don't think of as "apps" are, in fact, APPS. For example, if you drive, most modern cars have applications that monitor the engine, and on the road, some signs and signals are controlled with software.

Application security (APPSEC) refers to the measures taken to identify and minimize security vulnerabilities in computer applications. This includes developing and testing security features to prevent unauthorized access and modification. Various hardware, software, and procedural approaches achieve this goal. Hardware measures might include routers that block access to a computer's IP address from the internet. Software measures may involve application firewalls that control permitted and prohibited activities. Procedures might include regular testing as part of an application security routine.

Why is Application Security So Important?

Application security is critical in cybersecurity because attackers often target software applications to gain access to sensitive data, disrupt business operations, or carry out other malicious activities. For example, hackers can exploit application vulnerabilities to attack other systems, steal data or compromise the entire network.

By ensuring that applications are secure, organizations can minimize the risks associated with cyber threats, protect sensitive information, and maintain the trust of their users.

Moreover, with the increasing use of cloud computing and mobile devices, the number of applications and the complexity of applications used by organizations have increased, making them more vulnerable to cyber threats. Therefore, application security has become even more critical as a critical aspect of the overall cybersecurity strategy.

Application Security Features

There are various types of application security measures that organizations can implement to safeguard their applications from security threats and attacks. Some of the common types of application security are:

- **Authentication**: When developers build an application, they ensure only authorized users can access it. Authentication procedures are used to verify that the user is indeed the person they claim to be. This is commonly done by asking users to provide a username and password when they login to an application.

- **Authorization:** To access and use the application, a user must first be authenticated and verified against a list of authorized users. This ensures that only validated user credentials match the approved user list. Authentication must occur before authorization.

- **Input Validation:** Ensuring the accuracy and validity of user input data is called input validation. This process helps prevent attacks like SQL injection, cross-site scripting, and buffer overflow attacks.

- **Encryption:** Encoding data so only authorized people can access it is known as encryption. Sensitive data can be protected from being accessed by unauthorized people and compromised in the event of a data breach by encrypting it.

- **Access Control:** Access control measures restrict access to the application and its resources based on user roles and permissions. Implementing access control measures can prevent unauthorized access, ensuring users only have access to the resources they need to perform their duties.

- **Error Handling and Logging:** Error handling and logging measures help detect and diagnose application issues. Logging events and errors makes it easier to identify issues and take corrective measures to prevent them from occurring.

- **Security Testing:** Security testing involves various measures, such as penetration testing and vulnerability assessments, to identify and mitigate security risks. Security testing can help identify application vulnerabilities and take corrective measures to mitigate the risks.

- **Application Firewalls:** Application firewalls monitor and filter incoming and outgoing network traffic to prevent attacks. Application firewalls can prevent cross-site scripting, SQL injection, and buffer overflow attacks by filtering traffic based on predefined rules.

- **Security Updates and Patches:** Regularly updating the application and its underlying software components with the latest security patches and updates can prevent attackers from exploiting vulnerabilities.

- **Compliance with Security Standards:** Following best practices and complying with relevant regulations and standards, such as HIPAA or GDPR, can ensure the application is secure and protected from various security threats and attacks.

Security Framework Reference to Application Security

The NIST 800 has a few notable publications that address application security and development. NIST SP 800-218, Secure Software Development Framework. Security controls also address the secure development of applications, such as SA-10, Developer configuration management. CIS Critical controls has CIS 6.

CIS Control 16 is focused on application software security and aims to provide a comprehensive framework for securing applications throughout their lifecycle. The control is divided into three main components.

AppSec Training & Resources

Application security is expansive. Each programming and scripting language has its genre of application security. Here are some training and certification resources for you to look into:

- (ISC)² Certified Secure Software Lifecycle Professional (CSSLP): This certification validates an individual's expertise in secure software development throughout the entire lifecycle. (https://www.isc2.org/Certifications/CSSLP)

- Coursera - Secure Software Design Specialization: Offered by the University of Colorado, this specialization covers secure software design principles, threat modeling, and secure coding practices.

(https://www.coursera.org/specializations/secure-software-design)

- GIAC Secure Software Programmer (GSSP) Certifications: GIAC offers secure software programmer certifications in Java and .NET to validate a professional's ability to write secure code. (https://www.giac.org/certifications/software-security)

- OWASP Top Ten Project: The Open Web Application Security Project (OWASP) Top Ten Project provides a list of the most critical web application security risks and associated resources for learning. (https://owasp.org/www-project-top-ten/)

- Pluralsight - Application Security Courses: Pluralsight offers a range of application security courses covering topics such as secure coding, vulnerability assessment, and web application security. (https://www.pluralsight.com/browse/software-development/application-security)

- Udemy - Web Application Security Courses: Udemy provides various courses on web application security, including secure coding practices, penetration testing, and vulnerability assessment. (https://www.udemy.com/topic/web-application-security/)

- SANS Application Security Training: SANS offers in-depth training courses focused on application security, including secure coding, DevSecOps, and web application penetration testing. (https://www.sans.org/application-security)

- Cybrary - Application Security Courses: Cybrary offers free online courses on application security, covering secure software development, mobile application security, and web application security testing. (https://www.cybrary.it/catalog/?category=application-security)

- LinkedIn Learning - Secure Coding Courses: LinkedIn Learning provides courses on secure coding practices, covering topics like input validation, data handling, and web application security. (https://www.linkedin.com/learning/topics/secure-coding)

- AppSecEngineer: AppSecEngineer is a platform that offers hands-on, practical application security training courses on topics such as DevSecOps, secure coding, and cloud security. (https://appsecengineer.com/)

CHAPTER 11

INCIDENT RESPONSE

Freshworks.com

> "There are only two different types of companies in the world: those that have been breached and know it and those that have been breached and don't know it."
>
> ~Ted Schlein

Incident Response (IR) in cybersecurity is a structured approach to detecting, analyzing, and responding to security incidents within an organization's network or computer systems. It involves a team of experts who work together to identify the nature and extent of the incident, contain its impact, and recover from any damage caused. The incident response aims to minimize the impact of security incidents, identify the root cause, and prevent future incidents from occurring.

What are Security Incidents?

Security incident refers to any breach or event that risks an organization's sensitive data or information systems. This can come in various forms, such as intentional cyberattacks by hackers or unauthorized users or even unintentional violations of security policies by legitimate users.

It's important to remember that security incidents can harm an organization's information confidentiality, integrity, and availability. To protect against such incidents, it's crucial to take preventive measures and be ready to respond effectively if they do occur. This way, organizations can safeguard their data and systems from potential damage, theft, or misuse.

Security Incidents Include (but not limited to):

- **Ransomware:** Ransomware is malicious software that can hijack a person's data or device and demand a ransom from the victim to release it. This can have severe consequences for individuals and companies as it may lead to losing important information and resources.

- **Phishing & social engineering:** Phishing & social engineering attacks are also common, and they involve attempts to trick recipients into sharing sensitive information, downloading malware, or transferring assets to the wrong people. These attacks can be especially dangerous because they often come from sources that appear to be trustworthy, such as a known individual or a credible organization.

- **Insider threats:** Insider threats can pose a risk to an organization's information security, and there are two types of these threats. The first type is malicious insiders, authorized users such as employees or business partners who intentionally compromise security. The second type is negligent insiders, authorized users who unintentionally compromise security by not following security best practices, such as using weak passwords or storing sensitive data in insecure locations.

- **Distributed Denial of Service (DDoS):** DDoS attacks are another type of security incident that can disrupt or shut down an organization's network or servers. Hackers use remote control of large numbers of computers to flood a target's resources with traffic, making them unavailable to legitimate users.

- **Supply chain attacks:** supply chain attacks involve infiltrating a target organization by attacking its vendors. This can involve stealing sensitive data from a supplier's systems or using a vendor's services to distribute malware. In one recent example, cybercriminals took advantage of a flaw in Kaseya's VSA platform to spread ransomware to clients under the guise of a legitimate software update.

Process and Steps of Incident Response (IR):

- **Preparation:** A well-defined plan is essential for responding to a security incident. The plan should outline detailed procedures for each team member, including their roles and responsibilities. It should also identify essential assets and communication channels to be utilized during the incident.

- **Identification:** The second step is to identify that a security incident has occurred. This can be done through automated alerts generated by security monitoring systems, employee reports, or other means. Once an incident has been identified, the incident response team should be alerted.

- **Containment:** The third step is to contain the incident to prevent further damage. This may involve isolating affected systems, blocking network traffic, or shutting down systems entirely. Again, the objective is to limit the impact of the incident and prevent it from spreading further.

- **Analysis:** After the incident is contained, the incident response team can begin to analyze the incident. The process includes gathering and examining data to identify the underlying issue that caused the incident and assess the extent of the harm caused. The team may use various tools and techniques, such as forensic analysis and log analysis, to collect and analyze data.

- **Remediation:** The fifth step is to remediate the incident by removing the threat and restoring systems to their normal state. This may involve removing malware, patching vulnerabilities, or restoring backup data. The goal is to ensure that the incident is fully resolved and that the affected systems function correctly.

- **Recovery:** The final step is to verify that normal operations have been restored and that the organization is fully protected from future incidents. This may involve conducting additional security testing or implementing new security controls to prevent similar incidents from occurring in the future.

Importance of Incident Response

In today's world, cyber-attacks are becoming more advanced and frequent. Organizations must be equipped to handle incidents swiftly and efficiently. IR can aid in detecting and responding to incidents before they harm the organization's reputation, finances, or important assets.

By having a well-defined and tested IR plan in place, organizations can reduce the time it takes to identify and contain security incidents, reducing the cost and impact of the incident. Additionally, effective incident response can help organizations identify and address vulnerabilities in their security controls, which can help prevent future incidents from occurring.

IR TEAMS AND ROLES

- **Incident Response Coordinator**: The coordinator is responsible for overseeing the incident response process, including coordinating communication between team members, ensuring that response procedures are followed, and reporting on the status of the incident.

- **Incident Handler**: The incident handler is responsible for investigating and containing the incident. They must be able to analyze logs, conduct forensic analysis, and determine the scope and severity of the incident.

- **Forensic Analyst:** The forensic analyst is responsible for conducting a detailed forensic analysis of the affected systems to identify the incident's root cause, preserve evidence, and document the incident for future reference.

- **Malware Analyst:** The malware analyst is responsible for analyzing any malware that may have been involved in the incident. They must be able to identify the type of malware, determine its behavior, and develop a strategy for removing it from affected systems.

- **Network Security Analyst:** As a network security analyst, it is their primary duty to observe and examine network traffic to prevent and detect potential security issues. They must be well-versed with network security tools and technologies like firewalls and intrusion detection and prevention systems.

- **Public Relations/Communications:** The public relations/communications specialist communicates with internal and external stakeholders, such as employees, customers, and the media, about the incident. They must provide accurate and timely information and manage the organization's reputation.

IR PLANNING AND PREPARATION

Planning and preparation are critical components of incident response in cybersecurity. An effective incident response plan can help organizations detect and respond to security incidents quickly and effectively, minimizing the impact of the incident and reducing the risk of future incidents.

Here are some key elements of planning and preparation for incident response:

- **Identify Critical Assets:** Identify the critical assets of your organization that are most vulnerable to security threats. This could include sensitive data, critical infrastructure, or high-value systems. Prioritize these assets based on their level of criticality to the business.

- **Develop Response Procedures:** Develop detailed response procedures for each type of security incident that could occur. These procedures should include the steps to be taken in each phase of the incident response process, including identification, containment, analysis, remediation, and recovery.

- **Establish Communication Protocols:** To effectively handle incidents, it's important to establish communication protocols. This involves identifying the key stakeholders and setting up communication channels and escalation procedures.

- **Train Incident Response Team:** Train the incident response team on the incident response plan and procedures. This includes regular training and drills to ensure the team is familiar with the plan and can respond effectively in a real incident.

- **Test and Update the Plan:** Regularly test the incident response plan to ensure it is effective and current. This includes testing the procedures, tools, and technologies used in incident response. Update the plan as needed to reflect changes in the organization's infrastructure or security environment.

- **Document and Store Information:** Document and store all information related to the incident response plan, including procedures, contact information, and incident reports. Ensure that this information is accessible to the incident response team and other key stakeholders in the event of an incident.

The tools used for incident response are in Chapter 4: Continuous Monitoring & Chapter 7: Network Security.

Security Framework Reference to Incident Response

CIS 17 is a cybersecurity framework developed by the Center for Internet Security (CIS) that focuses on Incident Response and Management. It is a set of guidelines designed to help organizations establish and maintain an effective incident response plan in the event of a security breach or incident. The framework provides a detailed roadmap for organizations to follow when responding to security incidents. In addition, it offers best practices and recommendations for preparing, detecting, containing, investigating, eradicating, recovering from, and reviewing security incidents. CIS 17 is a critical component of a comprehensive cybersecurity strategy and can help organizations minimize the impact of potential data breaches or other cyber-attacks.

The NIST 800 covers incident response in the IR family of security controls.

Incident Response Training & Resources

Incident response is its industry. All companies, certifications, and services bring millions of dollars built around incident response. Here are some resources:

- GIAC Certified Incident Handler (GCIH): This certification validates an individual's skills and knowledge in managing security incidents and understanding common attack techniques. (https://www.giac.org/certification/certified-incident-handler-gcih)

- SANS Institute - Incident Response Training: SANS offers various courses related to incident response, including computer forensics, network forensics, and threat hunting. (https://www.sans.org/curricula/incident-response)

- (ISC)² Certified Information Systems Security Professional (CISSP): Although not specifically focused on incident response, the CISSP certification covers various security topics, including security operations and incident management. (https://www.isc2.org/Certifications/CISSP)

- EC-Council Certified Incident Handler (ECIH): This certification covers the fundamentals of incident response, including incident handling methodologies, tools, and techniques. (https://www.eccouncil.org/programs/certified-incident-handler-ecih/)

- Coursera - IT Security: Defense against the digital dark arts: This course, offered by Google, covers various IT security topics, including incident response and computer forensics. (https://www.coursera.org/learn/it-security)

- Cybrary - Incident Response Courses: Cybrary offers free online courses on incident response, covering incident handling, digital forensics, and network defense. (https://www.cybrary.it/catalog/?category=incident-response)

- Udemy - Incident Response Courses: Udemy provides various courses on incident response, including threat hunting, digital forensics, and incident management. (https://www.udemy.com/topic/incident-response/)

- Pluralsight - Incident Response Courses: Pluralsight offers a range of incident response courses covering topics such as digital forensics, malware analysis, and network security monitoring. (https://www.pluralsight.com/browse/information-cyber-security/incident-response)

- LinkedIn Learning - Incident Response Courses: LinkedIn Learning provides courses on incident response, including digital forensics, network defense, and incident management.

(https://www.linkedin.com/learning/topics/incident-response)

- edX - Cybersecurity Incident Response: This course, offered by RIT, covers the fundamentals of cybersecurity incident response, including incident detection, analysis, and containment. (https://www.edx.org/course/cybersecurity-incident-response)

CHAPTER 12

Assessments

> "The quality of assessors is critical to the quality of the assessment result."
>
> ~Pearl Zhu, <u>Quality Master</u>

We've talked about applying all kinds of security features on systems and networks of systems. We've mentioned creating secure configurations, monitoring logs, adding access controls, and many other security features. But if we are in an environment with hundreds of systems with teams implementing the security on all the systems, how do we know which systems have those security controls installed?

The best way to know if your system is secure is to assess it. An assessment is where the organization evaluates how effective the security best practices have been implemented.

There are many kinds of assessments to do this:

- Risk Assessments are used to score the overall security risk of the organization. These broad assessments can include other assessments to determine the likelihood of a threat to exploit a system's exposed weaknesses.

- Network assessments include internal, external, and DMZ scans to determine whether network security has been implemented throughout the enterprises.

- Privacy impact assessments determine what controls must be implemented to protect personally identifiable information.

- Physical security assessments look at how the assets are being protected. They look at the buildings, security cameras, entry and exits.

These are just a few of the kinds of assessments that are used. The type of assessment chosen depends on what security controls need to be evaluated.

Penetration testing, commonly called "pen testing," is a type of network assessment with techniques that involve simulating an attack by a malicious actor using the same tools and techniques as actual attackers. This exercise aims to identify and demonstrate the business impacts of vulnerabilities in a system.

Assessments are not all technical; besides physical assessments that look at fencing and alarm systems, some assessments thoroughly evaluate policies, processes, and procedures.

The Security Assessment Process

The security assessment process is a systematic approach to evaluating an organization's information security posture, identifying potential vulnerabilities, and ensuring the implementation of appropriate security controls. This process helps organizations protect their information systems, networks, and assets against security threats and maintain compliance with relevant regulations and standards.

The security assessment process typically consists of several key steps:

1. Scope definition: Determine the extent and boundaries of the assessment, including which systems, networks, applications, and assets will be evaluated. This step also involves identifying the relevant regulatory requirements and security standards that the organization must adhere to.

2. Data collection and analysis: Gather information about the organization's security posture, policies, procedures, and controls. This can include reviewing documentation, conducting interviews with relevant personnel, and examining system configurations. The collected data is then analyzed to identify gaps or weaknesses in the organization's security practices.

3. Risk assessment: Identify and analyze potential threats and vulnerabilities impacting the organization's information systems and assets. This involves assessing each identified risk's likelihood and potential impact and prioritizing them based on their overall risk level.

4. Security testing: Perform various security tests, such as vulnerability scans, penetration tests, or code reviews, to validate the identified vulnerabilities and assess the effectiveness of the implemented security controls.

5. Reporting: Document the findings from the security assessment, including identified vulnerabilities, risks, and gaps in the organization's security posture. The report should also provide recommendations for addressing these issues and improving the organization's security.

6. Remediation: Develop and implement a plan to address the identified vulnerabilities and risks. This may include updating security policies, revising system configurations, implementing new security controls, or providing additional personnel training.

7. Re-assessment: Periodically reassess the organization's security posture to ensure that the implemented security measures remain effective and to identify any new vulnerabilities or risks that may have emerged. This step helps maintain a strong security posture and demonstrates a commitment to continuous improvement.

By following this security assessment process, organizations can better understand their security risks, implement appropriate security controls, and ultimately enhance their overall security posture.

Security Framework Reference to Assessment

NIST 800 has the control family, RA, and risk assessments. But some documents walk the cybersecurity assessor through the process, NIST 800-53A, Assessing Security and Privacy Controls in Information Systems and Organizations & NIST 800-115, Technical Guide to Information Security Testing and Assessment.

Center for Internet Security (CIS) is a leading authority on cybersecurity. They provide Critical Security Controls (CIS Controls) guidelines that help organizations protect their systems and networks. One of these controls, CIS Control 18, stresses the importance of conducting penetration testing.

Assessment Training & Resources

There are a lot of resources and training programs for risk assessment:

- Certified Information Systems Auditor (CISA): This certification, offered by ISACA, validates an individual's skills and knowledge in auditing, assessing, and managing IT risk. [CISA Certification] (https://www.isaca.org/credentialing/cisa)

- SANS Institute - Risk Management Training: SANS offers various courses related to risk management, including security risk assessment, security policy development, and threat modeling. [SANS Risk Management Training] (https://www.sans.org/curricula/security-policy)

- Coursera - Information Security: Context and Introduction: This course, offered by the University of London, covers various information security topics, including risk management and risk assessment. [Information Security: Context and Introduction] (https://www.coursera.org/learn/information-security-data)

- (ISC)^2 Certified Information Systems Security Professional (CISSP): Although not specifically focused on risk assessment, the CISSP certification covers various security topics, including risk management and information security governance. [(ISC)^2 CISSP] (https://www.isc2.org/Certifications/CISSP)

- ISACA Certified in Risk and Information Systems Control (CRISC): This certification validates an individual's ability to identify, assess, and manage IT risk across an enterprise. [CRISC Certification] (https://www.isaca.org/credentialing/crisc)

- Udemy - Risk Assessment Courses: Udemy provides various courses on risk assessment, including IT risk management, security risk assessment, and business continuity planning. [Udemy Risk Assessment Courses] (https://www.udemy.com/topic/risk-assessment/)

- Cybrary - Risk Management Courses: Cybrary offers free online courses on risk management, covering topics such as risk assessment, security policy development, and business continuity planning. (https://www.cybrary.it/catalog/?category=risk-management)

- Pluralsight - Risk Management Courses: Pluralsight offers a range of risk management courses, covering topics such as risk assessment, security policy development, and IT risk management. (https://www.pluralsight.com/browse/information-cyber-security/risk-management)

- LinkedIn Learning - Risk Assessment Courses: LinkedIn Learning provides courses on risk assessment, including IT risk management, security risk assessment, and business continuity planning. (https://www.linkedin.com/learning/topics/risk-assessment)

- FAIR Institute: The FAIR Institute offers resources and training on Factor Analysis of Information Risk (FAIR), a framework for understanding, analyzing, and quantifying information risk in financial terms. (https://www.fairinstitute.org/)

Penetration testing can be a part of risk assessment, but it is its own thing:

- Offensive Security Certified Professional (OSCP): This certification is highly regarded in the penetration testing field, validating an individual's skills in performing hands-on security assessments. (https://www.offensive-security.com/pwk-oscp/)

- EC-Council Certified Ethical Hacker (CEH): This certification covers various hacking methodologies, tools, and techniques ethical hackers use to identify and remediate vulnerabilities. (https://www.eccouncil.org/programs/certified-ethical-hacker-ceh/)

- Coursera - Cybersecurity Specialization: This specialization, offered by the University of Maryland, covers various cybersecurity topics, including software security, network security, and penetration testing. (https://www.coursera.org/specializations/cyber-security)

- SANS Institute - Penetration Testing Training: SANS offers various courses related to penetration testing, including network penetration testing, web application penetration testing, and exploit development. (https://www.sans.org/curricula/pen-testing)

- GIAC Penetration Tester (GPEN): This certification validates an individual's skills in conducting penetration testing using ethical hacking methodologies and tools. (https://www.giac.org/certification/penetration-tester-gpen)

- Cybrary - Penetration Testing Courses: Cybrary offers free online courses on penetration testing, covering topics such as ethical hacking, network penetration testing, and web application penetration testing. (https://www.cybrary.it/catalog/?category=penetration-testing)

- Udemy - Penetration Testing Courses: Udemy provides various courses on penetration testing, including ethical hacking, network penetration testing, and web application penetration testing. (https://www.udemy.com/topic/penetration-testing/)

- Pluralsight - Penetration Testing Courses: Pluralsight offers a range of penetration testing courses covering topics such as ethical hacking, network penetration testing, and web application penetration testing. (https://www.pluralsight.com/browse/information-cyber-security/penetration-testing)

- LinkedIn Learning - Penetration Testing Courses: LinkedIn Learning provides courses on penetration testing, including ethical hacking, network penetration testing, and web application penetration testing. (https://www.linkedin.com/learning/topics/penetration-testing)

- Pentester Academy: Pentester Academy offers hands-on, practical training courses on penetration testing, network security, web application security, and other cybersecurity topics. (https://www.pentesteracademy.com/)

Conclusion

Continuous Learning

There are many best security practices that we didn't include, such as encryption, physical security, data loss prevention, supply chain security, threat intelligence, and mobile device management. Furthermore, emerging technologies like artificial intelligence, blockchain, augmented reality, and quantum computing will eventually need to be added to your knowledge base. Cybersecurity is a very broad field. Any of the topics discussed is an entire industry in and of itself, with its best practices, requirements, and exceptions.

For this reason, cybersecurity requires continuous learning and awareness of the technology. You must take the time to read new articles, listen to podcasts, watch videos, and take training on new technologies, threats, and vulnerabilities. One of the things that is exciting about this field is that it is ever-changing and has an influence on all IT, both old and new. So, keep learning!

Made in United States
Orlando, FL
12 July 2024

48893459R00075